MW01204177

A Teacher's Window Into the Child's Mind

and papers from the

INSTITUTE FOR NEURO-PHYSIOLOGICAL PSYCHOLOGY

by

Sally Goddard

A non-invasive approach to solving learning and behavior problems.

FERN RIDGE PRESS
EUGENE, OREGON
U. S. A.

Copyright @ Sally Goddard. All rights reserved.
No part of this book may be used or reproduced in any form
whatsoever without written permission from the author,
except in the case of brief quotations embedded in critical
articles or reviews.

Publisher's Data in Publication

Goddard, Sally, 1957-
A teacher's window into the child's mind. Eugene, Oregon, Fern Ridge Press. 1996.
144 p. 10 in, il., Index.
1. Child development. 2. Learning disabilities. 3. Reflexes - testing. 4. Developmental
Neurophysiology 5. Behavior disorders in children. 6. Educational psychology.
LC4818   370.15   ISBN 0 - 9615332 - 5 - 0

Printed in the United States of America
by Thomson-Shore, Inc., Dexter, MI 48130
Typeset electronically by
Editing & Design Services, Inc.
Child illustrations by Dan Chen

Fern Ridge Press,
1927 McLean Blvd
Eugene, OR 97405
(541) 485-8243 FAX (541) 687-7701

Dedicated to my Father

William D. Pritchard
1913 - 1995

"The good teacher does not bid you enter the house of his wisdom, but rather leads you to the threshold of your own mind."

Kahlil Gibran 'The Prophet'

Table of Contents

Chapter 5

Chapter 6

Appendix

ACKNOWLEDGEMENTS

To Peter Blythe, who started this work in 1969 and established The Institute for Neuro-Physiological Psychology in 1975. He has provided inspiration, education and encouragement to students, professionals and colleagues for over 20 years, given hope to children and their parents. The techniques used by INPP have now spread to the other side of the world and continue to develop in the light of new knowledge and research. The guiding hand remains that of its founder and director. "Between the idea and the reality is the creator."

Catherina Johanneson-Alvegård, who first developed this work in Sweden.

Dr. Kjeld Johansen.

Dr. Larry Beuret, Jane Field, Thake Hansen-Lauff, Bjorn Gustaffson Hakaan Carlson and Joan Young.

Prof. Birger Kaada whose work on the *Fear Paralysis Reflex* provided the missing link.

To many, many other people whose silent work, discussion and ideas have contributed to the development of this book.

To Svea Gold without whom this book would never have been written.

PREFACE

The American public is certainly the most educated generation on brain research since the Egyptians first wrote a papyrus on the brain in 1700 BC. In the early eighties, a twelve hour long video series "The Brain" provided every household with information gathered over the last 50 years. This series was followed with further programs on "The Mind" which connected what is happening in the brain with the personality of its owner. And more recently, "The Brain: Our Inner Universe." incorporated later information. New research is often reported on the News.

Nevertheless, to the layman the concept of a 'reflex' is only a very vague one. We might have a slight recollection of Pavlov's dog salivating at the sound of a bell. Our only contact with reflexes, however, might be when the doctor hits a child's knee with a hammer to see how well the reflexes work.

We may know a little about a 'gag reflex' or the quick reflexive intake of breath when a cold shower follows a warm one. But the idea that reflexes have an impact on the learning capabilities of a child is a new and —to most of us— strange idea.

As the British physiologist Sir Charles Sherrington stated: *"A simple reflex is probably a purely abstract conception, because all parts of the nervous system are connected together and no part of it is probably ever capable of reaction without affecting and being affected by various other parts, and it is a system certainly never absolutely at rest."*

It is this complexity that makes reflexes such excellent roadmaps to show what is happening in the brain without resorting to MRIs and PET scans. It is also what makes their use as a form of neurological recapitulation so very effective.

At the Institute for Neuro-Physiological Psychology, in Chester, England, Peter Blythe and Sally Goddard have found that reflexes provide accurate insight to a person's neurological organization. Not only do they provide clues as to what steps to take to help children with problems, but they also provide a means of therapy to restore function that may not have developed properly, and then — after therapy— a method of evaluating what progress has been achieved .

Brain researchers can essentially be divided into two groups. Those who observe children and learn from the functioning of 'normal' children, and those who do terrible things to crickets, cats, monkeys and chick embryos, in the hope of finally being able to help children. Only recently, the introduction of non-invasive MRIs, PET scans and CAT scans, has made it possible to explore — without surgery or autopsies— the secrets of what makes the brain affect man.

As a result, the nineties has a been called the 'Decade of the Brain' but its research has been built mainly on the work of the last twenty or thirty years. In 1986 Rita Levi-Montcalcini won the Nobel prize for her work with nerve growth factors (NGF). Since then over 100 of these have been discovered and classified. In the late seventies, researchers knew that specific movements would cause changes in the brain, but they did not understand how these changes were achieved. Today, hardly a week goes by without some new understanding of why this happens. We know of netrins - molecules which guide axons to their destination, or turn others away. We know of other chemical markers, collapsin, connectin and semaphorin, which guide or repel nerve fibers into their necessary paths. We know about pioneer cells and seem to have the ability to coax more neurons into a specific area of the brain.

All these recent discoveries add further pieces to the puzzle as to how the brain works. And yet, instead of this knowledge making the brain seem less magical, the more we know, the more exciting the miracle of its functioning becomes.

What all this knowledge proves, however, is that the therapy offered by using the reflexes of a child is not black magic but has a basis in the structure and the chemistry of the brain. Yet the intent of such therapy is to help — not to provide an abstract statistical number of cells in a lab dish.

The use of evaluating reflexes and using them in therapy is to give the child a well organized brain that allows it to learn efficiently and successfully.

Svea J. Gold
November 1995

INTRODUCTION

In our modern competitive world, academic achievement tends to be regarded as an essential ingredient for future success. Despite the changing methods in education and demands of the outside world, the percentage of children suffering from learning difficulties has remained largely unchanged since the 1970's. The term 'learning difficulties' has widened to encompass an overwhelming number of conditions. These may range from brain damage at one extreme, through autism, dyspraxia, dyslexia and low IQ., and finally to minor difficulties in specific subjects at the other end of the spectrum. Within this vast range of categories are a group of children who are to all appearances normal, but who fail to benefit from classroom teaching, and despite remedial teaching remain with their specific learning difficulties unresolved.

The following chapters describe a neuro-developmental approach to assessing and tackling the riddle of learning difficulties. If a student has failed to benefit from teaching strategies, then it is time to examine the neurological equipment of the child, to see if there is a physical basis underlying the poor academic performance. A neuro-developmental approach concentrates upon assessing the functioning of three systems fundamental to academic learning:

1. The reception of information through the sensory channels.
2. Processing of sensory information in the brain.
3. The repertoire of responses available to the child with which to express himself: motorically, linguistically and academically.

We must check if the child can control and voluntarily direct his responses, or if he is still governed by primitive patterns of response which only permit him to have immature reactions. Such reaction would interfere with higher more complex skills, because if there are problems in the underlying organization of the brain, any connections that are dependent on this organization will carry inherent weaknesses within them.

Detection of underlying problems is vital if a child is to receive relevant remedial help. Methods of assessment and of treatment are now available to correct developmental delay, improve the processing of sensory information and provide the child with more mature patterns of response. Only then will the skills of reading, writing and spelling become easy for him. The following chapters outline how this can be done and describe the theory and mechanics behind such methods.

Chapter 1

REFLEXES –
Their Impact on Success
or Failure in Education

When a child is born, he leaves the cushioning and protection of the womb to enter a world where he is assailed by an almost overwhelming amount of sensory stimuli. He cannot interpret the sensations that envelop him. If they are too strong, or too sudden, he will react to them, but he does not understand his own reaction. He has exchanged a world of equilibrium for one of chaos; he has left warmth for heat and cold. Automatic sustenance is no longer available and he must start to participate in feeding himself. No longer furnished with oxygen from the mother's blood, he needs to breathe for himself, and he must start to seek and to find the fulfillment of his own needs.

To survive, he is equipped with a set of primitive reflexes designed to insure immediate response to this new environment and to his changing needs. Primitive reflexes are automatic, stereotyped movements, directed from the brain stem and executed without cortical involvement.

Conscious awareness is possible only when the cortex becomes involved in the event.

They are essential for the baby's survival in the first few weeks of life, and they provide rudimentary training for many later voluntary skills. The primitive reflexes, however, should only have a limited life-span, and having helped the baby to survive the first hazardous months of life, they should be inhibited or controlled by higher centers of the brain. This allows more sophisticated neural structures to develop, which then allow the infant control of voluntary response.

If these primitive reflexes remain active beyond 6-12 months of life, they are said to be aberrant, and they are evidence of a structural weakness or immaturity within the central nervous system (CNS). Prolonged primitive reflex activity may also prevent the development of the succeeding postural reflexes, which should emerge to enable the maturing child to interact effectively with his environment. Primitive reflexes, retained beyond six months of age may result in immature patterns of behavior or may cause immature systems to remain pre-valent, despite the acquisition of later skills. One parent described his child as "having an infant still active within a ten-year-old's body."

Perception is the registering of sensory information in the brain.

Cognition is the interpretation and understanding of that information.

Inhibition - suppression of one function through the development of another. The first function becomes integrated within the second.

Disinhibition occurs after trauma or in Alzheimer's disease when reflexes re-emerge in their reverse chronological order.

Depending on the degree of aberrant reflex activity, this poor organization of nerve fibers can affect one or all areas of functioning: not only gross muscle and fine muscle co-ordination, but also sensory perception, cognition and avenues of expression.

The fundamental equipment essential for learning will be faulty or inefficient despite adequate intellectual ability. It is as if later skills remain tethered to an earlier stage of development and instead of becoming automatic, can only be mastered through continuous conscious effort.

The primitive reflexes emerge in utero, are present at birth, and should be inhibited by 6 months of age —12 months at the latest.

Inhibition of a reflex frequently correlates with the acquisition of a new skill. Thus knowledge of reflex chronology and normal child development may be combined to predict which later skill may have been impaired as a direct result of retained primitive reflexes. In much the same way that the parent used the analogy of an infant remaining active in a schoolboy's body, it may be said that the individual's aberrant reflexes can give us clues as to what is actively hindering later skills.

Detection of primitive reflexes can help to isolate the causes of a child's problem so that remedial training can be targeted more effectively. If the reflex profile is only marginally abnormal, teaching strategies *alone* will usually be sufficient. Children with a moderate degree of reflex abnormality may benefit from a combination of specialized teaching and some motor training, designed to improve balance and coordination. If, however, a **cluster** of aberrant reflexes are present, *neuro-developmental delay* is said to exist. In such cases, the child will only be able to sustain long term improvement after following a *reflex inhibition program* designed specifically for him to treat the aberrant reflexes still present.

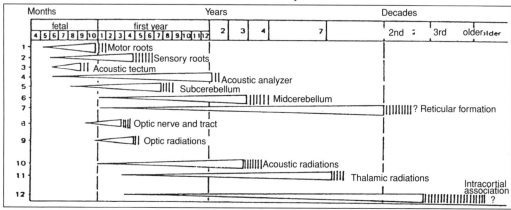

Figure 1: Periods of Intensive Myelination in Different Neural Systems — From before birth to beyond the third decade of life. — *from The Brain by Mildred Robeck*

A *reflex inhibition program* consists of specific physical, stereotyped movements practiced for approximately five to ten minutes per day over a period of nine to twelve months. The movements involved are based upon a detailed knowledge of reflex chronology and normal child development. Thelan (1979) observed that all human babies make a series of stereotyped movements during their first year of life. The Institute for Neuro-Physiological Psychology in the United Kingdom and Sweden, maintain that specific movement patterns made in the first months of life contain within them a natural inhibitor to the reflexes, and that if a child has never made these movements in the correct sequence, the primitive reflexes may have remained active as a result. By the application of stylized sequential movements, practiced daily, it is thus possible to give the brain a "second chance" to register the reflex inhibitory movement patterns which should have been made at the appropriate stage in development. As aberrant reflex activity is corrected, many of the physical, academic and emotional problems of the child will disappear.

Reflex —
an involuntary response
to a stimulus and the
entire physiological
process activating it.

Each reflex has a vital part to play in setting the stage for later functioning. In order to understand what goes wrong when reflexes become aberrant, it is important to realize what job individual reflexes perform at the time that their presence is normal. To do this, we need to return to the earliest weeks of an embryo's life—just five weeks after conception.

At this time the embryo starts to show signs of response to external stimuli. Gentle touch to the upper lip will cause the embryo to **withdraw** immediately from the stimulus — in an amebic-like response. Only a few days later, this area of sensitivity will be spread to include the palms of the hands and the soles of the feet, until eventually the whole body surface is responsive to touch. At this stage, however, the response is always one of **withdrawal** from the source of contact,

Fig. 2 —

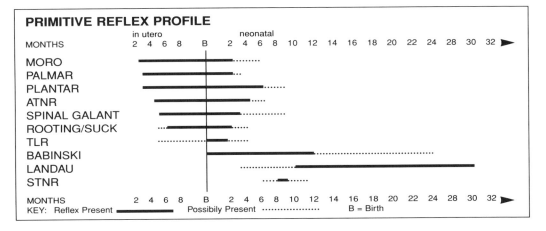

3

Neural development —not chronological age— determines at what time each reflex emerges and at what time it becomes inhibited. Thus the presence or absence of reflexes at key stages in development may be used as diagnostic signposts of central nervous system (CNS) maturity.

and is a total body reaction. As tactile awareness develops, withdrawal upon contact gradually lessens.

It is when the withdrawal reflexes are gradually lessening, estimated at 9 weeks in utero, that the first of the primitive reflexes emerge. The Moro reflex appears at 9-12 weeks after conception and continues to develop throughout pregnancy so that it is fully present at birth.

MORO REFLEX

Emerges: 9 weeks in utero
Birth: fully present
Inhibited: 2-4 months of life

TRIGGERS TO THE MORO REFLEX:

1. **Sudden, unexpected occurrence of any kind**
2. **Stimulation of the labyrinth by change in head position (Vestibular)**
3. **Noise (Auditory)**
4. **Sudden movement or change of light in the visual field (Visual)**
5. **Pain, temperature change, or being handled too roughly (Tactile)**

PHYSICAL RESPONSE TO THE MORO REFLEX.

1. **Instantaneous arousal**
2. **Rapid inhalation, momentary "freeze" or "startle"
    followed by expiration—often accompanied by a cry**
3. **Activation of "fight or flight" response, which auto-
    matically alerts the sympathetic nervous system and
    results in :**
    - A. **release of adrenaline and cortisol into the system
      (The stress hormones)**
    - B. **increase in the rate of breathing, particularly in
      the apices (upper lobes) of the lungs
      (Hyperventilation)**
    - C. **increase in heart rate**
    - D. **rise in blood pressure**
    - E. **reddening of the skin**
4. **Possible outburst, e.g. anger or tears**

LONG TERM RESPONSE

Poorly developed CO_2 reflex
The CO_2 reflex causes spontaneous inhalation of the upper and lower part of the lungs. When CO_2 levels become too high in the blood, chemical changes take place in the medulla, which will then open the arteries to increase blood supply to the brain and at the same time stimulate deep breathing.

The Moro reflex is a composite series of rapid movements made in response to sudden stimuli. It consists of a sudden symmetrical movement of the arms upward—away from the body—with opening of the hands, momentary freeze and then a gradual return of the arms across the body into a clasping posture. Abduction is accompanied by a sudden intake of breath. Adduction facilitates the release of that breath. Moro in 1918 emphasized his belief that it is essentially a "grasping" reflex, analogous to the one seen in young apes who instinctively cling to their mothers. He called it "Umklammerungsreflex" which literally translated means clasping reflex.

Abduction: opening of the arms and legs outward

Adduction: closing of the arms and legs as if to embrace or to clasp

The Moro reflex is an involuntary reaction to threat. The baby cannot yet analyze incoming sensation to assess whether that threat is real or not. The brain stem releases an immediate Moro response as if an emergency trip-switch were triggered automatically. It acts as the earliest form of "fight or flight" response and may be triggered occasionally in later life in situations of extreme danger. Essentially, however, it should be inhibited in its crude form from 2 to 4 months of age.

Its role as a survival mechanism in the first months of life is to alert, to arouse and to summon assistance. It is also thought to play a major part in developing the baby's breathing mechanism in utero, coinciding with

5

the earliest breathing-like movements observed in the womb. It facilitates the first "breath of life" at birth (encouraged by the midwife"s smack on the bottom or by holding the baby upside down by its feet) and helps to open the windpipe if there is threat of suffocation.

If the Moro reflex fails to be inhibited at 2-4 months of life, the child will be hypersensitive in one or several sensory channels, causing him to over-react to certain stimuli. Sudden noise, light, movement or alteration of position or balance—any of these—may elicit the reflex at unexpected moments, so that the child is constantly "on alert" and in a heightened state of awareness. The Moro-directed child is poised on the edge of fight or flight through most of his waking moments, caught up in a vicious circle in which reflex activity stimulates the production of adrenaline and cortisol—the stress hormones. These same hormones increase sensitivity and reactivity so that both the trigger and the response are built into the system. Such a child may present a paradox—acutely sensitive, perceptive and imaginative on the one hand, but immature and over-reactive on the other. He may cope in one of two ways: by being the fearful child who "withdraws" from situations, has difficulty in socializing, and can neither accept nor demonstrate affection easily. On the other hand, he may become the over-active, aggressive child, who is highly excitable, cannot read body language and who needs to dominate situations. Either child will tend to be manipulative, as he attempts to find strategies which will give him some measure of control over his own emotional responses.

Adrenaline and cortisol are two of the body's chief defenses against allergy and infection. If they are in constant use as "Leitmotif" in the child's life, they are diverted from their primary function, and there may be insufficient stores available to provide good immunity and balanced response to potential allergens. This may be the child who picks up every cough and cold in circulation and who over-reacts to certain medication. The child may be sensitive to certain foods or food additives, which in turn will affect behavior and concentration. He will also tend to burn up blood sugar quicker than other children, which will further exacerbate swings in mood and performance.

Stimulus bound: Inability to filter out and to ignore irrelevant sensory stimuli. Newborns watch reflexively anything that crosses their field of vision.

The child who still has a Moro reflex will experience the world as too full of bright, loud and abrasive sensory stimuli. The eyes will be drawn towards changes in light and to every movement within his visual field. His ears may receive too much auditory information. He cannot filter out or occlude extraneous stimuli, so he becomes easily overloaded. He is, in effect, "stimulus bound".

As Arnheim (1969) said, "Too many impressions which arrive from several sensory sources and which fall simultaneously on a mind which has not yet experienced them separately, will fuse for that mind into a single undivided object."

What then are the symptoms which a parent or a teacher might recognize as being suggestive of a strongly residual or retained Moro reflex?

LONG TERM EFFECTS OF RETAINED MORO REFLEX.

1.   **Vestibular related problems such a motion sickness, poor balance and coordination, particularly seen during ball games**
2.   **Physical timidity**
3.   **Oculomotor and visual-perceptual problems, e.g. Stimulus bound effect (cannot ignore irrelevant visual material within a given visual field, so the eyes tend to be drawn to the perimeter of a shape, much to the detriment of perception of internal features)**
4.   **Poor pupillary reaction to light, photosensitivity, difficulty with black print on white paper. The child tires easily under fluorescent lighting**

   In bright light the pupils should automatically contract to reduce the amount of light entering the eye. In dim light, they should rapidly dilate to allow maximum light to reach the retina. Failure to do this may result in photosensitivity and/or poor night vision.

5.   **Possible auditory confusion resulting from hypersensitivity to specific sounds. The child may have poor auditory discrimination skills, and have difficulty shutting out background noise.**
6.   **Allergies and lowered immunity, e.g. asthma, eczema, or a history of frequent ear nose and throat infections**
7.   **Adverse reactions to drugs**
8.   **Poor stamina**
9.   **Dislike of change or surprise—poor adaptability**
10.   **Poorly developed CO_2 reflex**
11.   **Reactive hypoglycemia**

*** While other residual reflexes tend to have an impact on specific skills, it is the Moro which has an overall effect on the emotional profile of the child. ***

POSSIBLE SECONDARY PSYCHOLOGICAL SYMPTOMS.

1.   **Free floating anxiety—"Angst" (continuous anxiety seemingly unrelated to reality)**
2.   **Excessive reaction to stimuli**
     A.   **Mood swings—labile emotions**
     B.   **Tense muscle tone (body armoring)**
     C.   **Difficulty accepting criticism, as this child finds it so difficult to change**
3.   **Cycle of hyperactivity followed by excessive fatigue**
4.   **Difficulty making decisions**
5.   **Weak ego, low self esteem**
     A.   **Insecurity/Dependency**
     B.   **Need to "control" or "manipulate" events**

As the earliest primitive reflex to emerge, the Moro reflex forms a corner-stone in the foundation for life and for living. It is essential for the neonate's survival, but its effects are profound if it fails to be inhibited at the correct time and transformed into an *adult startle response.*

The adult startle response consists of a quick shrugging movement, followed by a turn of the head to check for the source of the disturbance, and once that has been identified, the infant proceeds with whatever it was doing.

PALMAR REFLEX

(The infant grasp reflex)

Emerges: 11 weeks in utero
Birth: Fully present
Inhibited: 2—3 months of life

Transformed: Gradual development from involuntary grasp to release and refined finger control. Replaced by the pincer grip at 36 weeks of age.

The palmar reflex forms a part of the group of reflexes which develop in utero, and whose common characteristic is to "grasp." A light touch or pressure to the palm of the hand will result in closure of the fingers. By 18 weeks after conception the response will have extended to included a gripping reflex in response to a pull against the finger tendons. Both of these responses should strengthen during uterine life, to be fully developed at birth. They should be strongly active for the first 12 weeks of life and transformed by 4-6 months of life, so that the child can hold an object between his thumb and index finger in a pincer grasp grip. The ability to release an object follows some weeks later and must be practiced many times before the child can acquire good manual dexterity.

Both the palmar and the plantar reflexes are thought to be a continuation of an earlier stage in human evolution, when it was still necessary for the neonate to cling to its mother for safety. There is also a direct link between the palmar reflex and feeding in the early months of life. The palmar reflex can be elicited by sucking movements, and the action of sucking may cause kneading of the hands in time to sucking movements. (Babkin response) Both the mouth and the hands are the major sources of exploration and expression during the neonate period. Continued reflex activity in the area can have a lasting adverse effect upon fine muscle coordination, speech and articulation if they fail to be inhibited at the correct time.

The effects of this neurological loop which connects the palms with the movements of the mouth can often be seen when the child first learns to write or to draw. Until these skills come easily, the child will lick his lips, or twist his mouth some other way. Teachers will often admonish: "You"re not writing with your tongue!" Developmental optometrists call this "overflow" and consider the child to have made visual progress when this overflow disappears.

If the palmar reflex remains, the child cannot proceed through the subsequent stages of release and finger mobility. Gesell (1939) described the process as follows: *"Voluntary grasping, such as reaching, indicates a proximo-distal course of development. Early grasping consists of crude palming movements in which the three ulnar fingers predominate, whereas the thumb is practically inactive. This type of grasp is later succeeded by a refined fingertip prehension, characterized principally by thumb opposition, forefinger dominance, readiness for manipulation and the adaption of finger pressure to the weight of the object."* This can only occur as the palmar reflex becomes inhibited.

Proximo-distal: development of the infant's muscle control from the center outward.

LONG TERM EFFECTS OF A RETAINED PALMAR REFLEX.

Ulnar: first three fingers.

1. **Poor manual dexterity. The palmar reflex will prevent independent thumb and finger movements**
2. **Lack of "pincer" grip, which will affect pencil grip when writing**
3. **Speech difficulties— continuing relationship between hand and mouth movement via the Babkin response will prevent the development of independent muscle control at the front of the mouth, which will then affect articulation**
4. **Palm of the hand may remain hypersensitive to tactile stimulation**
5 . **Child makes movements with mouth when trying to write or draw**

A retained or residual palmar reflex beyond 4-5 months of life will impede both manual dexterity and manipulatory activities. Handwriting will be affected as the child will be unable to form a mature pencil grip. Speech may also be affected as a continuing relationship between hand and mouth movements will prevent the development of independent muscle control at the front of the mouth. Clear articulation may be just one casualty.

ASYMMETRICAL TONIC NECK REFLEX

Emerges: 18 weeks in utero
Birth: Fully present
Inhibited: About 6 months of life

Movement of the baby's head to one side will elicit reflexive extension of the arm and leg to the side to which the head is turned and flexion of the occipital limbs.

The asymmetrical tonic neck reflex (ATNR) has an active part to play from the time of its emergence in utero, until approximately six months of life. During uterine life, the asymmetrical tonic neck reflex should facilitate movement (the kick), develop muscle tone and provide vestibular stimulation.

Occipital limbs— arm and leg on the side to which the back of the head is turned.

9

The ATNR <u>in utero</u> provides continuous motion which stimulates the balance mechanism and increases neural connections.

It should be fully established by the time the fetus is ready to be born, so that it may participate in the birth process. Labor should not begin until the fetus has reached maturity, when mother and baby may then act as cooperative partners in the birth process. As the second stage of labor is achieved, the baby should help to "unscrew" itself down the birth canal in rhythm with the mother's contractions. The baby's active participation in this is dependent upon the presence of a full asymmetrical tonic neck reflex. The reflex is activated by the massaging effect of maternal contractions. When the baby's head presents, the midwife may turn the head gently from one side to the other, activating the asymmetrical tonic neck reflex, so that the baby eases its way down the final few inches of its hazardous journey. The birth process will also reinforce the asymmetrical tonic neck reflex (together with other reflexes) so that it is firmly established and active for the first months of life.

The ATNR not only assists the birth process but is reinforced by it. This may be one reason why children taken by Cesarean section are at higher risk for developmental delay.

During the neonate period, the asymmetrical tonic neck reflex (ATNR) ensures a free passage of air when the baby is in the prone position. It increases extensor muscle tone, training one side of the body at a time, and forms the basis for later reaching movements.

Prone—
lying on the tummy

Extensor—
stretching away from body

DeMyer (1980) describes the asymmetrical tonic neck reflex (ATNR) as *"the first eye-hand coordination to take place. It is present at the time that visual fixation upon nearby objects is developing, and it seems that the nervous system is making sure that the appropriate arm stretches out towards visualized objects. As the hand touches the object, the seeds of awareness of distance (at arm's length) and eye-hand co-ordination are sown."* (Holt, 1991)

By six months of age, the asymmetrical tonic neck reflex (ATNR) should have completed its task and the developing brain should release further movement patterns which contain the inhibitor to the asymmetrical tonic neck reflex, allowing more complex skills to be acquired. Continued presence of an asymmetrical tonic neck reflex (ATNR) will interfere with numerous functions. For example, it is impossible to crawl on the stomach with a fluent cross-pattern movement if the asymmetrical tonic neck reflex persists. Crawling and creeping are important for the further development of hand-eye co-ordination and the integration of vestibular information with other senses. Myelination of the central nervous system (CNS) is enhanced during these processes.

The child who still has an asymmetrical tonic neck reflex when he learns to walk may find his balance is insecure. Movement of the head to either side will result in straightening of the limbs on that side, upsetting the center of balance and insisting on homolateral movement.

If the child walks with the left hand swinging forward as the left foot moves forward, and conversely with the right hand moving at the same time as the right foot, the result will be a robot-like walk. This walk alerts other children to the fact that there is something different and makes the child an easy target for teasing. In sports, tasks such as throwing and kicking a ball will thus appear awkward and clumsy.

The retained asymmetrical tonic neck reflex will cause difficulty in crossing the midline from one side of the body to the other, so that the child cannot make the transition from merely grasping to manipulating an object with both hands. The child will also not be able to establish a preferred hand, leg or ear and if there is no dominant side, there will always be a slight hesitancy in the child's movements. He does not know, for instance, which hand to use to pick up a hammer, a pencil, or a ball. Since this choice does not become automatic, every movement has to be consciously made, and this becomes an unnecessary source of stress.

The 6 month old baby who still has this reflex will find it difficult to make the normal transition from being able to pass an object from one hand to the other. This skill is normally acquired at about 28 weeks. The asymmetrical tonic neck reflex becomes an invisible barrier to crossing the midline. The entire body will still want to execute tasks using one side at a time, and thus fluent interchange of bilateral movement will be impaired.

Eye movement will also be affected as the child will remain "stimulus bound" at the midline. When such a child is asked to follow an object as it is moved slowly in front of him on a horizontal line, there will be a slight hesitancy as the object is moved from one side of his nose to the other. This same hesitancy will also prevent fluency when he later tries to read.

It is only during the second half of the first year that the child starts to acquire good far-distance vision, and a retained asymmetrical tonic neck reflex may tether the child's vision to arm's length, preventing the next stage from proceeding. Tracking or "ocular pursuit" will also be impaired, with later effect upon reading, writing and spelling.

In the classroom, handwriting will be the most obvious casualty of a retained asymmetrical tonic neck reflex. Each time the child turns his head to look at the page, his arm will want to extend and the fingers will want to open. Thus, holding and manipulating a writing implement for any length of time, will require enormous effort. It is as if an elastic band is attached to the pencil and then tethered to the corner of the table. The child is thus fighting against a perpetual invisible force. He may learn to compensate by using an immature pencil grip or by using excessive pressure, but the physical act of writing will always require intense concentration at the expense of cognitive processing. Both the quality and quantity of handwriting will be affected. Writing may slope in different directions from one side of the page to the other. The child may rotate the page by as much as 90 degrees when writing in an attempt to "accommodate" the effect of the asymmetrical tonic neck reflex. Fluent expression of ideas in written form may show a marked discrepancy from the child's ability to express himself orally.

SYMPTOMS SUGGESTIVE OF A RESIDUAL OR RETAINED ASYMMETRICAL TONIC NECK REFLEX.

1. **Balance may be affected as a result of head movement to either side**
2. **Homolateral, instead of normal cross-pattern movements, e.g. when walking , marching, skipping, etc.**
3. **Difficulty crossing the midline**
4. **Poor ocular "pursuit" movements, especially at the midline**
5. **Mixed laterality. (Child may use left foot, right hand, left ear, or he may use left or right hand interchangeably for the same task.)**
6. **Poor handwriting and poor expression of ideas on paper**
7. **Visual-perceptual difficulties, particularly in symmetrical representation of figures**

ROOTING REFLEX

Emerges: 24-28 weeks in utero
Birth: Fully present
Inhibited: 3-4 months of life

Searching, sucking and swallowing reflex should be present in all full-term babies. They, also, form part of the group of "grasp" reflexes which develop in utero.

Light touch of the cheek or stimulation of the edge of the mouth will cause the baby to turn the head toward the stimulus, and open the mouth with extended tongue in preparation for sucking. This reflex may be elicited at all four quadrants of the mouth, and thus is sometimes referred to as the cardinal points reflex.

The combination of rooting and suck reflexes insure that the baby turns toward the source of food and opens his mouth wide enough to latch on to the breast or bottle. The sucking and swallowing movements which follow are vital for early feeding. Odent (1991) stated that the rooting reflex is at its strongest in the first couple of hours after birth, but if the baby does not receive gratification for his "rooting" attempts shortly after birth, the reflex will weaken. Premature babies who have to be incubated, can frequently be seen "rooting" for the first couple of days of life, but, unable to receive the appropriate response, the rooting reflex starts to diminish. In some of these children, the reflex can still be elicited in weakened form long after it should have been inhibited. In common with other reflexes, if it is not used fully at the correct time, it appears to behave rather like a Victorian spinster—unfulfilled, frustrated and unable to let go!

Retained or residual oral reflexes will result in continued sensitivity and immature responses to touch in the mouth region—particularly in the area of the lip. The infant may experience difficulty when solid foods are introduced, as a persistent suck reflex will prevent the tongue from developing the mature combination of movements necessary for swallowing, and remains too far forward in the mouth to allow effective chewing. Copious dribbling which continues into school age may be one result, as both reflexes prevent the child from gaining adequate control of the muscles at the front of the mouth. Manual dexterity may also be affected as immature sucking and swallowing movements continue to affect the hands, causing involuntary palming movements to occur in time with sucking. (Babkin response)

****

"The stimulus for this reflex consists of deep pressure applied simultaneously to the palms of both hands while the infant is an appropriate position, ideally supine. The stimulus is followed by flexion or forward bowing of the head, opening of the mouth and closing of the eyes. The reflex can be demonstrated in the newborn, thus showing a hand-mouth neurological link even at this early stage. It fades rapidly, and normally cannot be elicited after 4 months of age. Elicitation of the reflex after this age indicates a cerebral lesion." (Holt, 1991)

Any further indications of the hand/mouth neurological connection are called Babkin response. Like many other reflexive reactions, the effect can be seen in either direction, in this case from hand to mouth, or mouth to hand.

****

Swallowing, feeding, speech articulation and manual dexterity may all be casualties of residual or retained oral reflexes in the older child. As Roberta Shepherd said, *"The development of normal swallowing and of normal coordination between respiration and oral function are all essential elements in the development of speech. It is thought that the muscular action involved in feeding is an essential preparation for babbling and speech."* (1990)

**LONG TERM EFFECTS OF RETAINED ROOTING
AND SUCK REFLEXES.**

1. Hypersensitivity around lips and mouth
2. Tongue may remain too far forward in the mouth, which
    will make swallowing and chewing of certain foods
    difficult—the child may dribble. Lack of mature
    swallowing movements may cause increased arching of the
    palate (cathedral palate) and the need for orthodontic
    treatment later on.
3. Speech and articulation problems
4. Poor manual dexterity

SPINAL GALANT

Emerges: 20 weeks in utero
Birth: Actively present
Inhibited: 3-9 months of life

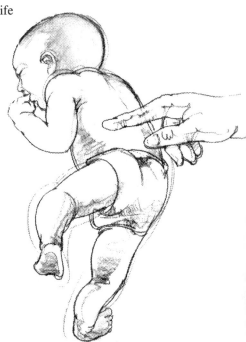

If the baby is held in the ventral or placed in the prone position,
stimulation of the back to one side of the spine will result in hip flexion
(rotation) to 45 degrees toward the side of the stimulus. It should be
present with equal strength bilaterally.

Little is know about the functions of the spinal Galant reflex, except that it may take an active role in the birth process. Contractions of the vaginal wall stimulate the lumbar region and cause small rotational movements of the hip on one side, similar to the head and shoulder movements of the asymmetrical tonic neck reflex. In this way, the baby can help to work its way down the birth canal.

Ventral :
Lying on tummy, head
and hips not supported.

It has been suggested (Dickson, 1991) that the Galant may act as a primitive conductor of sound in utero, allowing sound vibration to travel up through the body in the aquatic environment of the womb, enabling the fetus to "feel" sound, or assisting sound vibrations to travel up the spinal column.

If the spinal Galant reflex remains beyond the neonate period, it may be elicited at any time by light pressure in the lumbar region. Stimulation down both sides of the spine simultaneously will activate a related reflex, which will cause it to urinate. A retained or residual spinal Galant reflex, is found in many children who may have poor bladder control, and who continue to wet the bed above the age of 5 years. Beuret, (1989) working in Chicago with adults, has found it to be present in a high percentage of patients suffering from irritable bowel syndrome.

For the child in the class room, the most obvious effect of a retained spinal Galant reflex will be difficulty in sitting still for any length of time. This is the "ants in the pants" child who wriggles, squirms and constantly changes body position, as the elastic of the waistband or simply leaning against the back of a chair may activate the errant reflex. Understandably, the child may dislike clothing which is tight around the waist. The reflex may also affect concentration and short-term memory as this constant irritant is always vying for the child's attention.

If the Galant remains present on one side only, it may affect posture, gait and any other form of locomotion. This can result in the illusion of a "limp" or contribute to scoliosis. It may also interfere with the full development of the later amphibian and segmental rolling reflexes, affecting fluency and mobility in physical activities or sports.

SYMPTOMS OF A RETAINED GALANT REFLEX

Scoliosis :
abnormal curvature of
the spine

1. Fidgeting
2. Bedwetting
3. Poor concentration
4. Poor short term memory
5. Hip rotation to one side when walking.

TONIC LABYRINTHINE REFLEX

TONIC LABYRINTHINE REFLEX (TLR) FORWARDS

Emerges : in utero—flexus habitus
Birth: present
Inhibited: approximately 4 months of life

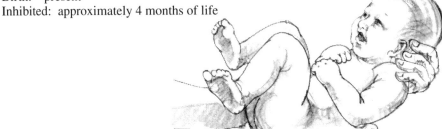

TONIC LABYRINTHINE REFLEX (TLR) BACKWARDS.

Emerges: at birth
Inhibited: gradual progression
from 6 weeks of age up to 3 years
of age, involving the simultaneous
development of postural reflexes,
symmetrical tonic neck reflex and
the Landau reflex.

The Moro and tonic labyrinthine reflexes are closely linked in the early
months of life. Both are vestibular in origin, and both are activated by
stimulation of the labyrinths and therefore any alteration of position in
space. The tonic labyrinthine reflex (TLR) is elicited by movement of
the head forwards or backwards, above or below the level of the spine.
It is thought that flexus habitus (the position of the fetus in utero) is
the earliest manifestation of the tonic labyrinthine reflex in the forward
position. The tonic labyrinthine reflex should be fully present at birth.
Extension of the head below the level of the spine causes immediate
extension of the arms and legs. (Fig 9)

The tonic labyrinthine reflex should be fully developed in both
positions from birth. Inhibition of the tonic labyrinthine reflex forwards
should be accomplished by 4 months of life. Inhibition of the tonic
labyrinthine reflex backwards is a more gradual process, involving the
emergence of several postural reflexes and taking up to age 3 to be
completed.

Being born introduces the baby to an entirely new set of challenges. Hitherto, he has been in an enclosed aqueous environment, in which the effects of all sensory stimuli are cushioned, and the effect of gravity is reduced. The tonic labyrinthine reflex provides him with an early primitive method of response to the problem of gravity. Any movement of the head in 'a vertical direction beyond the midline will cause extremes of flexion or extension throughout the body to occur, influencing muscle tone from the head downwards. By 6 months of age, the response should be modified so that head control can develop, with the emergence of the oculo- and labyrinthine head-righting reflexes. Head control is an essential prerequisite for the development of all later functions and should be the prime initiator of early movement, tonus and balance. (Cephalo-caudal law)

The tonic labyrinthine exerts a tonic influence upon the distribution of muscle tone throughout the body, literally helping the neonate to "straighten out" from the flexed posture of the fetus and the newborn. Thus, balance, muscle tone and proprioception are all trained during this process.

Cephalo-caudal law: from head to toe downward sequence of development.

If the tonic labyrinthine reflex fails to be inhibited at the correct time, it will constantly "trip" the vestibular in its actions, and in its interaction with other sensory systems. The child who still has a retained tonic labyrinthine reflex when he starts to walk, cannot acquire true gravitational security, (Ayres, 1979-1982) as head movement will alter muscle tone, "throwing" the center of balance. Lacking a secure reference point in space, the child will experience difficulty in judging space, distance, depth and velocity. A sense of direction is based upon our knowledge of where we are in space—if our point of reference is fluctuating and unstable, then the ability to discriminate up from down, left from right and back from front may also be erratic. This is a condition experienced by astronauts in space. When astronauts are put into a gravity free environment, they start to write from right to left, to reverse numbers and letters and to produce "mirror-writing", demonstrating the significance of gravity and balance for all levels of functioning.

Continued tonic labyrinthine reflex activity will prevent the head-righting reflexes from developing fully. If the head control is lacking, eye functioning will also be impaired as the eyes operate from the same circuit in the brain—the vestibulo-ocular reflex arc.

If one segment of the circuit is malfunctioning it will affect the smooth operation of other systems dependent upon that circuit. Balance will be affected by faulty visual information and vision will be affected by poor balance. A two way system of "mismatch" may be established, which the child will assume to be normal because he has never known anything else.

The tonic labyrinthine reflex (TLR) may also prevent the child from being able to creep on his hands and knees, as movement of the head

17

Fig. 3 — Organization of the vestibular system

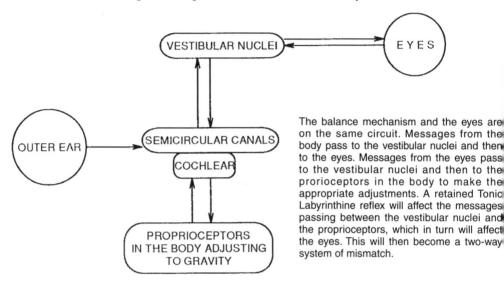

The balance mechanism and the eyes are on the same circuit. Messages from the body pass to the vestibular nuclei and then to the eyes. Messages from the eyes pass to the vestibular nuclei and then to the prorioceptors in the body to make the appropriate adjustments. A retained Tonic Labyrinthine reflex will affect the messages passing between the vestibular nuclei and the proprioceptors, which in turn will affect the eyes. This will then become a two-way system of mismatch.

will result in extension of the legs. The symmetrical tonic neck reflex (STNR) will also remain "locked" in the system in a futile attempt to over-ride the tonic labyrinthine reflex (TLR) preventing creeping on hands and knees. Crawling and creeping fulfill both training and inhibitory process. Both facilitate integration of sensory information as vestibular, visual and proprioceptive systems all start to operate together for the first time. During that period of developmental movement, the child acquires a sense of balance, a sense of space and a sense of depth. It is through crawling and creeping that the raw materials of seeing, feeling and moving synchronize for the first time to provide a more complete picture of the environment.

Prolonged influence of the tonic labyrinthine reflex (TLR) can have implications for many other areas of functioning. Balance and movement will be affected. Standing for any length of time may be tiring and posture may have to adjust in an attempt to accommodate the reflex. There may be overall "bowing" of the body or a tendency to stand with the head poked forward. The child may have very floppy muscle tone and appear either slovenly or seem to be jerky and stiff in his movements, particularly in walking, running or jumping. The child may develop a fear of heights as he is intrinsically aware of his poor balance, and the fact that movement of his head forwards will cause his knees to bend and create the sensation of falling forwards toward the drop. Holding his arms up will rapidly become tiring, and he will be acutely aware of changes in the level of the ground under his feet, as his feet will attempt to grip the ground as a method of maintaining equilibrium.

Resultant oculomotor dysfunction will cause the eyes to "play tricks" so that he cannot always rely on what he sees. Depth perception may be impaired and he may suffer from figure-ground effect.

****

Figure ground effect: The child cannot easily separate and categorize conflicting visual information. e.g. walking up an open staircase or crossing a slatted bridge, where the water can be seen through the boards. He may have difficulty getting his eyes to readjust from far to near distances, so that there is a temporary "blind spot" in the visual information he receives. Not only will abilities which require spatial perception be affected but he may also have difficulty locating sound and become easily disorientated.

****

Head control and good balance, are essential to the automatic functioning of all other systems—a residual tonic labyrinthine reflex (TLR) will prevent the complete establishment of both head control and of balance.

SYMPTOMS SUGGESTIVE OF A STRONGLY RESIDUAL TONIC LABYRINTHINE REFLEX FORWARDS

1. Poor posture—stoop
2. Hypotonus (weak muscle tone)
3. Vestibular related problems
    A. Poor sense of balance
    B. Propensity to get car sick
4. Dislike of sporting activities, physical education classes, running, etc.
5. oculomotor dysfunctions
    A. Visual-Perceptual difficulties
    B. Spatial problems
6. Poor sequencing skills
7. Poor sense of time

SYMPTOMS OF A STRONGLY RESIDUAL TONIC LABYRINTHINE REFLEX BACKWARDS

1. Poor posture—tendency to walk on toes
2. Poor balance and coordination
3. Hypertonus—stiff , jerky movements because the extensor muscles exert greater influence than the flexor muscles
4. Vestibular related problems
    A . Poor sense of balance
    B. Tendency to motion sickness
5. Oculomotor dysfunction.
    A. Visual-perceptual difficulties
    B. Spatial perception problems
6 . Poor sequencing skills
7. Poor organization skills

SYMMETRICAL TONIC NECK REFLEX

(STNR) **Flexion**.

Emerges: 6-9 months of life.
Inhibited: 9 -11 months of life.

When the child is in the quadruped position, flexion of the head causes the arms to bend and the legs to extend.

(STNR) **Extension**.

Emerges: 6-9 months of life.
Inhibited: 9 -11 months of life.

Head extension, on the other hand, causes the legs to flex and the arms to straighten.

The symmetrical tonic neck reflex should have a very short life-span. It helps the baby to defy gravity by raising up—on to hands and knees from the prone position. Capute (1981) has suggested that it may not be a true reflex, but a crucial stage of the labyrinthine reflex. It certainly facilitates inhibition of the tonic labyrinthine reflex (TLR) and it forms a bridge to the next stage of locomotion—creeping on hands and knees. However, while it permits the child to assume the quadruped position, it will prevent forward progress in this position. The baby will be at the mercy of its head movement, unable to move effectively because during this period of development the position of the head decides the position of the limbs. (Bobath and Bobath, 1955)

Gesell described progression through the early postural reflexes thus:
"At 20 weeks the supine infant can roll over on his side by rotating the upper portion of the body and then flexing the hips and throwing the legs to that side. (segmental rolling reflex) This accomplishment represents the first gross shift in body posture. At 28 weeks, the child can attain a crawling position, (full arm extension and amphibian reflex) and sustain the weight of the upper portion of the body by one or both arms. He can bring one knee forward beside the trunk, but cannot raise his abdomen. Locomotion begins at about 32 weeks. The

child pivots about by means of his arms. He succeeds in raising himself to the crawling position at 36 weeks, (symmetrical tonic neck reflex) but cannot progress on his hands and knees until 44 weeks. It is at this stage that the contralateral arm and leg movements begin."

Bending of the legs as a result of head extension (head lifted above spine) will assist in inhibition of the tonic labyrinthine reflex. It will also encourage the infant to "fixate" his eyes at far-distance. Bending of the arms in response to flexion of the head (head lowered below the spine line) will automatically bring the child's focus back to near-distance, thus training the eyes to adjust from far to near distance and back again. It has been suggested (Blythe, 1992) that the symmetrical tonic neck reflex (STNR) helps to complete a sequence of eye training. The asymmetrical tonic neck reflex (ATNR) begins by extending the baby's ability to focus from about 7 inches (17 cm) at birth, to arms length. As the asymmetrical tonic neck reflex (ATNR)is inhibited at about 6 months of age, the field of vision is extended to distant objects. The symmetrical tonic neck reflex (STNR) then brings the vision back to near-distance once more, training the readjustment of binocular vision. It remains for the process of creeping on hands and knees to develop the visual skills the infant has learned so far, and to integrate them with information from other senses.

Fixate: focus eyes on stationary point

Creeping is one of the most important movement patterns to help the eyes cross the midline, as they focus from one hand to another, with the hands acting as moving stimuli. This ability is essential for being able to read without losing the words at the middle of the line. It is through creeping that the vestibular, proprioceptive and visual systems combine to operate together for the first time. Without this integration there would be no sense of balance, space and depth.

Creeping: crawling on hands and knees

The focusing distance and hand-eye coordination skills used in the act of creeping are at the same distance that the child will eventually use for reading and writing. It has been observed (Pavlides, 1987) that a high percentage of children with reading difficulties omitted the stages of crawling and creeping in infancy.

Crawling: crawling on tummy

Studies of certain primitive tribes have revealed that they possess remarkable visual acuity at far distance, but that they have never developed a written language of their own. The Xinguana Indians can fire a dart from a blow pipe with deadly accuracy as far as half a mile, but they cannot read or write. Within the jungle terrain in which they live, the children spend most of their first year carried upon their mother's body. The ground is fraught with danger from poisonous insects, snakes and plants. Consequently, they are never allowed to learn to crawl or to creep on the ground. Veras (1975) maintains there is a strong connection between crawling and creeping and the ability to comprehend and to use a written language. *"Not only is creeping an important level of development in a child's mobility, it is also terribly important in the child's visual development. In all the primitive people we have seen, the children are never allowed to creep, and none of them can focus his eyes on anything closer than arms length. They are all far sighted. We believe that when a child creeps, his near-point vision is developed."*

Rosanne Kermoian and her colleagues conducted a study at Reed College in 1988 and found that many cognitive skills, such as object permanence and space perception are learned during the creeping period—and not until then.

Although the symmetrical tonic neck reflex (STNR) enables the baby to get up off the floor, it does not permit mobility in the quadruped position. Normally babies pass through a period of "rocking" on hands and knees, which gradually inhibits the symmetrical tonic neck reflex. If the symmetrical tonic neck reflex (STNR) remains strongly active, then creeping may not ensue. The baby may learn to "bottom hop" or to "bear-walk", or one day he may simply get up and walk.

In the older child, the influence of the symmetrical tonic neck reflex may be seen in a stooped posture, severe slouching, or gradual bending of the arms when sitting at a desk, as head flexion (lowering his head) will cause the arms to bend or collapse. This is the child who ends the lesson almost lying on the desk in order to write.

The child with a symmetrical tonic neck reflex may be the clumsy child who has difficulty coordinating hand and eye movements, dreads physical education classes and is a disaster at ball games. He may lose sight of the ball in motion and by the time he has perceived it at near distance again, it is too late to hit or to catch with any degree of accuracy. Basic skills such as eating may be messy, as the hand never quite seems to be in the right place to find the mouth. Posture at the table, also, will be poor.

SYMPTOMS SUGGESTIVE OF A STRONGLY RESIDUAL SYMMETRICAL TONIC NECK REFLEX.

1. **Poor posture**
2. **Tendency to "slump" when sitting, particularly at a desk or table**
3. **Simian (ape like) walk**
4. **"W" leg position when sitting on the floor**
5. **Poor hand-eye coordination**
   A. Messy eater
   B. "Clumsy child" syndrome
6. **Difficulties with readjustment of binocular vision .**
   (Child cannot change focus easily from black board to desk.)
7. **Slowness at copying tasks**
8. **Poor swimming skills**

Chapter 2

FROM PRIMITIVE REFLEX TO POSTURAL CONTROL

If it is the primitive reflexes which lay the foundations for all later functioning, then it is the postural reflexes which form the framework within which other systems can operate effectively. The transition from primitive reflex reaction to postural control is *not an automatic one.* There are no set times at which the later reflex asserts control over the earlier one, but it is a gradual process of interplay and integration during which both reflexes operate together for a short period of time.

The movements made because of the reflex action myelinize brain circuitry in much the same way that the road network of a country is laid out.

As certain movement sequences are practiced over and over again, more mature patterns of response can supersede primitive reflexive response.

This period of growth, change and elaboration operates rather like an interweaving spiral, through which nature ensures that primitive survival patterns are still accessible until such time as more mature postural reactions are becoming automatic.

THE POSTURAL REFLEXES

Postural reflexes are mediated from the level of the midbrain, and their development thus signifies the active involvement of higher brain structures over brain stem activity, and are a sign of increased maturity in the central nervous system (CNS). Some posturals are educationally significant.

They comprise two groups:
1. The Righting Reflexes (Quadruped)
2. Equilibrium Reactions (Bipedal)
   (Fiorentino 1981).

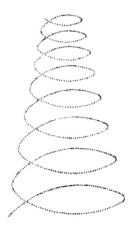

Both are concerned with posture, movement and stability. The righting reactions emerge at 3-12 months of age, and should remain present throughout life until disease or old age intervene. They enable the child to maintain his head and trunk in a specific position when the body position is altered in any way. Their emergence facilitates movement through rolling, crawling and creeping, and later will permit coordinated gross motor movement to take place.

Righting reactions consist of the oculo-headrighting reflex, the labyrinthine headrighting reflex, the amphibian reflex, Landau reflex and segmental rolling reflexes.

Equilibrium reactions are controlled by the cortex, first appearing at approximately 3-6 months of age and persisting throughout adult life.

They comprise the protection and tilting reactions which are elicited if balance is lost, or the center of gravity altered. They include the *"startle"* (also known as Strauss) reflex and the *parachute* reflex.

> *Educationally, their presence is not of immediate significance, except that <u>absence</u> of equilibrium reactions suggest immaturity of the Central Nervous System. Socially, however, the impact may be enormous. Because the child will appear clumsy and uncoordinated, he will invite teasing and may become isolated from the group. Organizational skill will also suffer, because balance will be affected, and the resultant dizziness interferes with concentration.*

The Strauss reflex develops as the Moro reflex is inhibited and it acts as the adult startle response. The child tenses the muscles, blinks, seeks out the source of danger and then makes a cortical (conscious) decision about how to react. The adult startle response may be seen as the result of the completion of three developmental stages:

1. WITHDRAWAL REFLEX

Uterine ⟶ This is an extreme reaction to "startle" resulting in immediate shut down or shock response—immobility, slowing of the heart rate, drop in blood pressure, cessation of breathing and extreme fear.

2. MORO REFLEX

Primitive ⟶ This is a primitive over-reaction to "startle", which results in stimulation of the sympathetic nervous system—increase in heart rate, immediate rise in blood pressure, rapid, shallow breathing, flushing of the face, accompanied by anger or distress. A Moro reflex which is only partially inhibited can result in "body armoring" in an attempt to control the over-reaction.

3. STRAUSS REFLEX

Postural ⟶ Mature response to "startle", involving cortical analysis of the situation.

Postnatal motor development takes place in a cephalo-caudal (head to toe) and proximo-distal (center outward) sequence. The development of postural reflexes should reflect this pattern. The first task a child must accomplish is mastery of head control and muscle tone, before further controlled voluntary movement can occur. Control is gained in the prone position before supine. By six weeks of age, the child can raise his head in line with his body when lying prone, and can hold it in that position for several seconds. By twelve weeks, he can lift his head well above the general body line and maintain it there for several minutes. By twelve weeks his legs are no longer flexed and his pelvis is flat on the surface when lying prone. By sixteen weeks he can press down with his forearms to lift his head and upper torso, stretching his limbs and "swimming" in this position.

muscle tone:
balance between flexor
and extensor muscles.

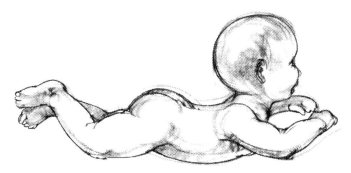

Swimming in prone

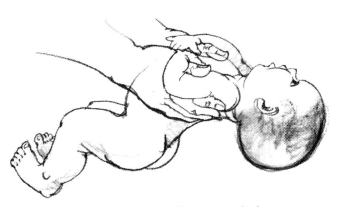

Head lag in supine position at 1 month of age

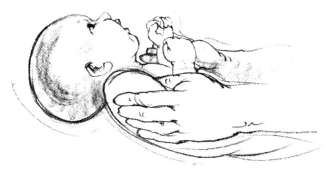

Head control to the midline at 3 months of age

25

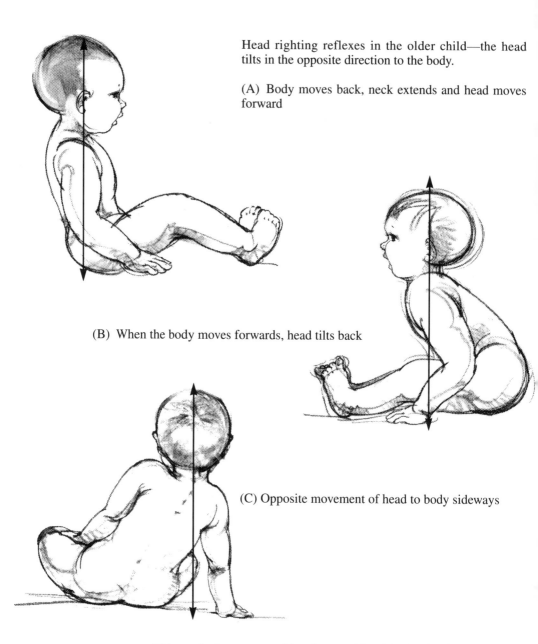

Head righting reflexes in the older child—the head tilts in the opposite direction to the body.

(A) Body moves back, neck extends and head moves forward

(B) When the body moves forwards, head tilts back

(C) Opposite movement of head to body sideways

This gradual sequence of head control heralds the development of the oculo- and labyrinthine headrighting reflexes. Together these ensure that the head maintains a midline position despite movement of other parts of the body either actively or passively induced. The oculo-headrighting reflexes operate as a result of visual cues, while the labyrinthine headrighting reflexes are dependent upon vestibular information. The two should synchronize to supply accurate data upon which head position is adjusted. If they fail to develop fully, or only one develops adequately, balance, controlled eye movements and visual perception will all be impaired. Muscle tension in the neck and shoulder region combined with poor posture may therefore be symptoms of underdeveloped headrighting reflexes, as the 44 pairs of muscles in the neck responsible for holding the head up, fight to maintain head control without the support of automatic righting reactions. There is a lag in attaining head control in the supine position which means that the infant is approximately 5 months of age before he can raise his head and hold it for some time above the level of the spine, in this position.

THE LANDAU REFLEX

The Landau reflex has a relatively short life span, emerging at the same time as the headrighting reflexes at 3-10 weeks of age, and being inhibited by the age of approximately 3 years. The Landau reflex elicits extensor tone throughout the body in the prone position if the baby is suspended in the air with support under the stomach.

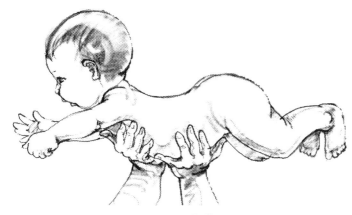

Landau Reflex

Neither the Landau nor the symmetrical tonic neck reflex are true primitive or postural reflexes. They are not present at birth and therefore cannot be categorized as primitive, but neither do they remain present for the remainder of life and therefore are not true postural reflexes. They seem to act as important "bridge" reflexes which have an inhibitory effect upon the tonic labyrinthine reflex, strengthen muscle tone and develop vestibulo-ocular motor skills.

Development of the Landau reflex helps to increase muscle tone when prone. Simultaneously it acts as an inhibitory influence upon the tonic labyrinthine reflex (TLR) forwards, increasing headrighting, and muscle tone in the torso. It enables the child to elevate not only the head but also the chest, and is an important prerequisite for more advanced movements involving the arms and hands later on. By 3 years of age, by which time the child should be secure as a mobile biped, the Landau reflex should no longer be necessary. Its continued presence in later life suggests underlying primitive reflex activity, and will affect development of balance and of voluntary alteration of muscle tone in rapidly changing conditions, e.g. a child may run with stiff awkward movement in the lower half of the body, and find hopping, skipping and jumping difficult as he cannot flex the leg muscles at will.

THE AMPHIBIAN REFLEX

The amphibian reflex should develop at 4-6 months of life, first in prone, then in supine. Elevation of the pelvis elicits automatic flexion of the arm, hip and knee on the same side.

Flexion of one leg irrespective of head position permits an increase in mobility and marks an important stage for the development of crawling on the tummy. Hitherto, flexion or extension of the legs bilaterally has been dependent upon head position and has been determined by the activities of the asymmetrical tonic neck reflex (ATNR). The amphibian reflex thus denotes significant inhibition of the ATNR. Freedom from this constraint permits the independent movement of the legs and arms essential for crawling, creeping and gross muscle coordination later on.

> *An __underdeveloped__ amphibian reflex will impede cross pattern crawling and creeping and may contribute to hypertonus in later life thus interfering with activities dependent upon gross muscle coordination e.g. physical education, sports, etc. Total lack of an amphibian reflex suggests uninhibited primitive reflexes, particularly the asymmetrical tonic neck reflex (ATNR) and the tonic labyrinthine reflex (TLR).*

SEGMENTAL ROLLING REFLEXES

These are sometimes also referred to as the "neck on body and body righting reactions". To produce a segmental roll, they should develop at two key positions in the body; the shoulders and the hips. Movement starts at the head, then follows to the shoulders, thorax and pelvis or vice versa.

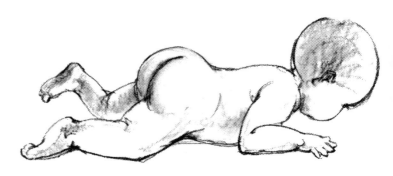

Prone to supine

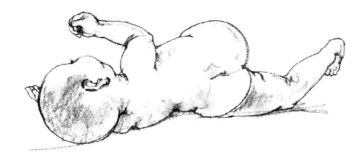

Supine to prone

These reflexes start to emerge at 6 months of age to allow rolling, first from prone to supine at 6 months, then from supine to prone at 8-10 months, followed by sitting, four point kneeling and eventually standing. As the child becomes practiced and adept at these activities, the reflex becomes redundant for progress from lying to standing, but should remain through life to facilitate changing positions and to give fluidity to movements such as running, jumping, skiing etc.

EQUILIBRIUM REACTIONS

These are protective reactions which occur in response to a sudden alteration in position or when balance is lost. They are dependent upon visual stimulation, and it has been suggested that they are linked to the adult "startle" or Strauss reflex. (Fiorentino, 1981)

The parachute reflex may be elicited if the infant is held in the air and then tilted forward toward the ground. The arms extend as if to protect the head and trunk from the full force of impact. If the infant is held upright and dropped rapidly toward the ground, the lower limbs first extend, tense then abduct. The reflex's value is a protective one.

At approximately 6 months of age the sideways parachute or "propping" reflex also emerges. This is essential if a child is to learn to sit, since it provides for any loss of balance in the sitting position by compensatory movement of the arm on the side to which the child is falling, "propping" the trunk and preventing the infant from toppling over. This reflex should be present during the child's early attempts at standing, cruising and walking.

*** There are many other reflexes which play an essential role in the development and well-being of the individual. The few which have been selected here for discussion in their relationship to education, may be elicited through standard neurological tests and can be seen to be of direct significance to the child who is failing in the classroom. ***

Chapter 3

BRAIN DEVELOPMENT

Absent or underdeveloped postural reflexes have long been accepted as contributory factors in coordination problems and associated disorders, such as dyspraxia, "clumsy child" syndrome, apraxia, etc. With this in mind, motor training programs have been devised to encourage the development of postural reflexes, and thus improve coordination and balance. Some of these, such as what has become known as the Doman-Delacato program, are based on the concept that brain organization has an impact on learning problems and can be changed by repeating early developmental movements.

Glenn Doman and Carl Delacato have long since gone in their separate directions. Their techniques have evolved and improved over the years and their methods should not be evaluated by what they advocated twenty-five years ago. Carl Delacato has also pioneered in the treatment of autistic children.

The techniques employed in sensory integration (A. Jean Ayres) are based upon the concept that stimulation of the postural reflexes through specific physical exercises can encourage the development of more mature patterns of response and will also suppress underlying primitive reflex activity. General improvement in balance and coordination demonstrate the value of such programs, particularly where the source of the problem lies in lack of postural reflexes with only minimal primitive reflex activity still present.

If the primitive reflexes are still strong, however, stimulation of postural reflexes alone will rarely reap concomitant changes in the areas of fine muscle coordination, oculomotor functioning, perceptual processing and academic performance. This may be because, while motor training programs strengthen postural control, they fail to inhibit those retained primitive reflexes which continue to impede the processing of information in the brain. In order to understand why this may be the case, we need to examine some of the mechanisms within the brain, and how they develop during the first year of life.

Establishing a hierarchy :

The brain comprises many separate entities which are all interlinked and dependent upon each other. At birth, connections to the superficial layers of the cortex are only tenuously made, and the neonate is a brain stem dominated creature.

The brain stem is situated at the head of the spinal column and houses the nerve pathways which carry impulses between the brain and the body. It is part of the central nervous system (CNS) and is responsible for the neurons which control heart beat, blood pressure, breathing and also the signals to swallow, laugh, sneeze, etc. It forms the evolutionary

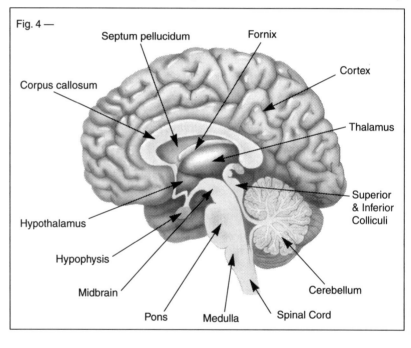

Fig. 4 —
Septum pellucidum   Fornix
Corpus callosum
Cortex
Thalamus
Superior & Inferior Colliculi
Hypothalamus
Hypophysis
Midbrain
Cerebellum
Pons   Medulla   Spinal Cord

core or primitive site, which is shared by man, fish and reptile. The function it fulfills is so fundamental that injury to the core of the brain stem results in death. The brain stem also contains the point at which the nerve tracts between brain and the body cross over and change course to the opposite side. The brain stem includes the pons and medulla oblongata. Linked to it, is the vital reticular formation, which is responsible for maintaining consciousness and arousal.

The reticular activating system (RAS) is like the brain's own alarm clock, monitoring sensory signals and passing them through to alert or "calm down", according to the circumstances.

Forming a bridge between the brain stem and the cortex lie the pons and the midbrain. These centers, as well as the thalamus, basal ganglia and hypothalamus,—and then the cerebellum—interact to form the organization centers of the sensory, motor and autonomic systems.

RAS —
A complex network of nerve fibers, occupying the central core of the brain stem, that function in wakefulness and alertness

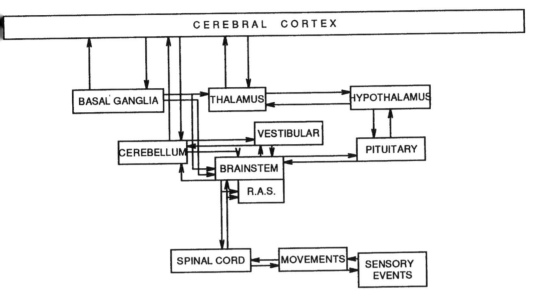

FIG 5 — CORTICAL CONTROL

The thalamus acts as an important relay station which carries impulses from the cerebellum, reticular system and neural ganglia to the cortex. All of the senses with the exception of smell are filtered through the thalamus before they reach their specialized regions in the cortex, and it therefore plays a vital role in the potential interpretation of sensory stimuli.

The hypothalamus is situated slightly below the thalamus and acts as the synthesizer of the hormones involved in temperature control, water balance, hunger and sexual behavior. These hormones are then funneled into the pituitary gland where they are stored or released into the bloodstream. These two centers together are labeled the seat of the limbic system which man has in common with other mammals. It is from the limbic system that sensation, passion, drive, fear, anger and grief are all generated. If the brain stem represents survival, then it is the midbrain and the limbic system which represents what we call instinct, and which largely controls our metabolism and our metabolic reactions to the outside world.

It has been suggested (Gaddes, 1980) that some behavior results directly from reflexive or spontaneous stimulation of the hypothalamus and related structures, combined with inhibitory learned processes emanating from the cerebral cortex. *"Too much hypothalamic stimulation with too little cortical (or intellectual) control presumably results in the socially obnoxious child who disregards the rights and wishes of others. The reverse pattern may result in the overcontrolled, inhibited, unimaginative child."* This sounds remarkably similar to the two profiles which are characteristic of the Moro directed child described in Chapter 1.

The basal ganglia are responsible for the organization of involuntary and semivoluntary activity, upon which consciously willed movements are superimposed. It should therefore maintain the balance between inhibitory and facilitating influences. Activities which at first need practice should eventually be absorbed into the automatic repertoire of the basal ganglia. Learning to play the piano, learning to drive a car or ride a bicycle, would fall into that category.

Basal Ganglia— three small masses of nerve tissue involved in the subconscious regulation of movements

Connected to the brain stem, but not a part of it, is the cerebellum. Its name literally means "the little brain"—because of its two hemispheres.

While it is the cerebral cortex which enables us to perform all the higher functions which are unique to mankind, it is the cerebellum which governs man's every movement. Although it can initiate nothing by itself, the cerebellum monitors impulses from the motor centers in the brain and from the nerve endings in the muscles. Incoming impulses outnumber efferent impulses 3:1 for it is the cerebellum's job to sift out and to pass on relevant information. Impulses to the cerebellum are directed from the vestibular system, the eyes and the muscle joints of the lower limbs and trunk. Ultimately, the cerebellum is responsible for regulating the postural reflexes and muscle tone, and thus maintaining the body's equilibrium.

Fig. 6 —

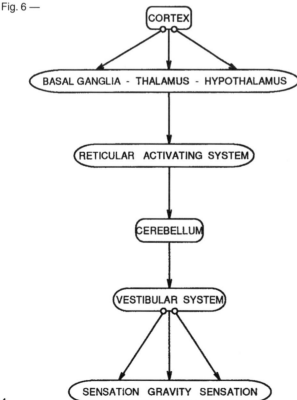

The smooth operation of the motor system is dependent upon the entire central nervous system, both motor and sensory. Voluntary and semi-voluntary movement develop through practice, but are not possible without pre-existing postural patterns which are already established by the basal-reticular system. As the child approaches maturity, the order of command should function from the top downward with the cerebral cortex influencing and modifying the action of the basal ganglia, which in turn modifies centers of the brain stem, then modifying the cord reflexes. At every level there is a feedback of information to the centers, and the cerebellum acts as the vital monitor in this feedback network. Dysfunction at any level releases centers below from the influences of those above. Equally, failure of lower centers to be inhibited will prevent higher centers from maintaining control. The chain of command should resemble the diagram on the next page (Fig. ?).

34

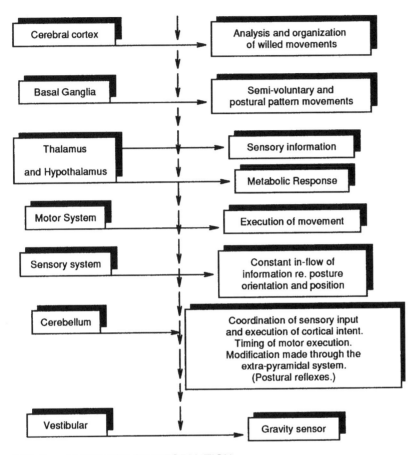

FIG. 7 — FEEDBACK OF INFORMATION

Cerebellar damage can cause paralysis in affected regions of the body. Cerebellar dysfunction can result in clumsiness affecting visualmotor performance and manual dexterity. Hence the cerebellum used to be known as "the patron saint of the clumsy child." (Restak 1991) As the regulator of the postural reflexes, cerebellar-dependent functions will be profoundly affected if the postural reflexes fail to develop. Equally, cerebellar dysfunction may prevent the development of postural reflexes. The cerebellum also plays an important role in sequential and rote learning, and in short term memory. This may be one reason why medication aimed at the cerebellum and the vestibular apparatus (Levinson, 1984) dramatically improves the performance of some dyslexic children.

Finally, at the top of the brain pyramid is the cerebral cortex, comprising two hemispheres which are linked together by the corpus callosum. Although some tasks are shared by both hemispheres, the left and right side of the cerebral cortex have specialized functions to perform, but are dependent upon each other for the execution of those tasks, hence the significance of the corpus callosum between them. The corpus callosum contains millions of nerve fibers which facilitate communication and instantaneous feedback from one side of the brain to the other. For example, if the two sides of the cortex were chemically or surgically separated, and the patient asked to pick out two previously identified faces in a large crowd, each side would use a different method. The left side of the brain would laboriously search every face one by one in logical sequence until it found the face it was looking for. The right brain would scan the sea of faces until it alighted on the target, but the owner of the brain could not tell us their name, since connection to the language center in the left hemisphere has been cut. Communication between the two sides is obviously of vital importance.

> *One of the major differences between men and women can be seen here, as the corpus callosum develops to be 40% larger in women than in men. This may go some way to explaining man's tendency to be more "single minded" in his approach to tackling problems, while the woman can be aware of a number of factors simultaneously. It is in the cortex that information passed on from all the other brain centers becomes conscious, and on the basis of cortical analysis, decisions for action will be made. The cortex should be the seat of intellect, of decision and of controlled response, but it can only do its job easily and effectively if the reflexive action of the lower centers are integrated at the correct time, in a hierarchical sequence.*

The corpus callosum also seems to act as a screening device, at times shielding information between the two sides of the cortex. It should be capable of either transmitting or inhibiting exchange of information.

HEMISPHERIC SPECIALIZATION

In addition to having specific skills, the right hemisphere of the cortex seems to play an important part in the learning of new tasks. In a sense it is the "practice ground" for newly acquired skills, which will then defer to the left hemisphere to apply dissection, logic and detail. When a certain level of understanding or attainment has been reached, one side of the brain can become the "specialist" for that task. Bakker (1990) maintains that a child should learn to read in this way: *"In initial reading, the balance of brain activity favors the right hemisphere, whereas advanced readers favor the left hemisphere. Thus, there is a moment in the learning to read process at which the balance in the brain tips from right to left at approximately the age of $6^1/_2$-$7^1/_2$ years."*

This is the same age at which a major period of myelination and "linking" takes place between the vestibular apparatus, the cerebellum and the corpus callosum. Is it not then a quantum leap to suppose that a child's reading readiness, is closely linked to his neuro-developmental age? Developmental age may not necessarily be parallel with chronological age and the teaching methods should be chosen taking the child's developmental stage into consideration.

Fig. 8

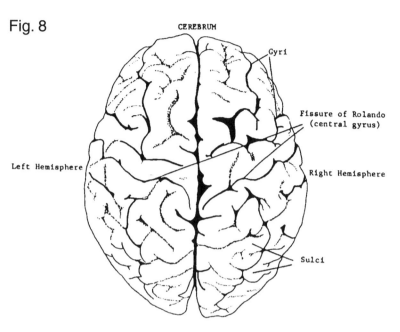

CEREBRUM

Gyri

Fissure of Rolando
(central gyrus)

Left Hemisphere

Right Hemisphere

Sulci

Right hemisphere reading is based on visio-spatial and holistic skills, e.g. whole words, or "look-say" method.

Left hemisphere reading involves decoding of individual symbols, word building from letters, and phonetics based skills.

Victims of left hemisphere damage demonstrate severe speech and language problems. One young man who had been in a ghastly car accident in his early 20's and suffered severe left hemisphere damage as a result, was able to describe what it felt like for him: *"I no longer see sound as I used to. Sound for me is a flat map; there are no hills and valleys although I know there once were. I know what I want to say but the words are like Everest and I cannot see the top."* His speech was flat, monotone, stuttering and without cadence. He was attempting to use the sublanguage center of the right hemisphere to communicate, and the result was like that of an adult making first attempts at a foreign language. Many children who are left-ear dominant demonstrate some form of language difficulty either in speech or written spelling. Galaburda's (1978) research on the brains of dyslexics shows that a high percentage have abnormally small left hemispheres, suggesting either lack of left hemisphere development from the outset, or underdevelopment through lack of use.

In the Far East, where the written language is based on pictograms, dyslexia barely exists. Much of Eastern philosophy is also based on right hemisphere thinking, i.e. the ability for past, present and future to coexist simultaneously. When we dream, we also do this, so that logically disconnected events can be brought together and viewed through visio-spatial, holistic representation.

Dyslexics appear to favor right hemisphere methods of learning. When reading, writing and spelling, they have difficulty applying left hemisphere techniques. This is unfortunate, because such usage might further enhance left hemisphere maturation.

Unilaterality:
dominance of one
side of the cortex
over the other.

Homolateral:
one side of the body
at a time. i.e. arm and
leg on one side of the
body move together.
In the adult this may
cause a soldier to be
unable to march, or
the dancing partner
to seem to have two
left feet.

Dysdiadochokinesia:
difficulty with rapid
alternate movement,
e.g. fine muscle
movement in the
hands, finger or feet.
This will affect
handicraft activities
and may also be
linked to speech
defects.

Continued presence of the asymmetrical tonic neck reflex (ATNR) interferes with unilaterality of brain function. (Gesell & Ames 1947, Telleus, C.1980) This results in homolateral patterns of movement and causes a midline barrier to cross-pattern movements of the body, and also slows speed of transmission within the brain.

Difficulties with dysdiadochokinesia are symptomatic of lack of cerebral dominance, or put another way, until the cerebellum has mastered control of fine muscle movements so that the child can perform the finger-opposition test without difficulty, independent movement of each side of the body has not been established, and cerebral dominance has not occurred.

The greatest period of growth and of maturation occurs in the cerebellum between birth and 15 months of age, just the period when the adjustments from primitive reflex to postural control are being made. Maturation continues at a slower rate until the age of seven or eight years, when the final "linking" takes place between the vestibular apparatus, the cerebellum and the corpus callosum. It is generally accepted that occasional letter, number and word reversals when reading and writing are normal up until the age of approximately eight years just the time when this final linking should have taken place. Continued reversal after this age may not be merely symptomatic of a dyslexic type of problem, but may also be suggestive of vestibular/cerebellar immaturity with implications for many other areas of functioning. Lack of postural reflexes would confirm this diagnosis.

The term "triune brain" (MacLean, P., 1979) describes the brain as being divided into three levels. Each level embodies or represents a stage in evolution. The brain stem symbolizes the "reptilian brain", because it is shared by all vertebrates from reptile to man. In his early weeks of life, the neonate is a totally brain stem dominated creature, and the movements that he makes are reptilian in character —head lift, squirming and rolling in a gravity bound world. The midbrain represents MacLean's "mammalian brain" and takes the young infant through the stages of rolling, crawling, sitting, creeping and standing. Finally, the cortex takes control, enabling us to stand and to move with independent use of the hands, and eventually to grow into rational, logical linguistic and altruistic human beings. All levels remain within us, but lower brain regions should not remain predominant. If they do, they will prevent the final stage of cortical control from being acquired completely.

Figs. 9-10-11

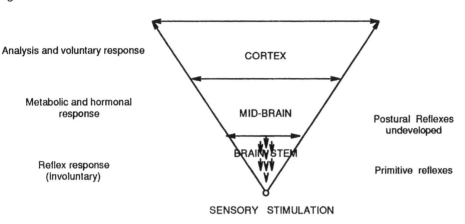

BIRTH TO FOUR MONTHS OF AGE

Analysis and voluntary response

CORTEX

Metabolic and hormonal response

MID-BRAIN

Postural Reflexes undeveloped

Reflex response (Involuntary)

BRAIN STEM

Primitive reflexes

SENSORY STIMULATION

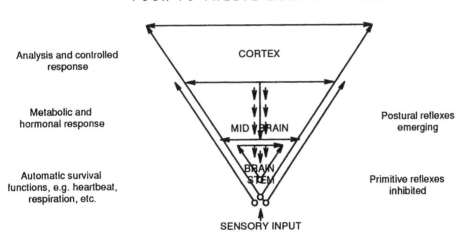

FOUR TO TWELVE MONTHS OF AGE

Analysis and controlled response

CORTEX

Metabolic and hormonal response

MID BRAIN

Postural reflexes emerging

Automatic survival functions, e.g. heartbeat, respiration, etc.

BRAIN STEM

Primitive reflexes inhibited

SENSORY INPUT

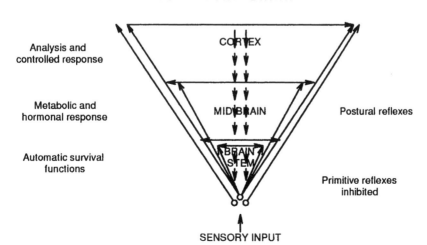

THE MATURE BRAIN

Analysis and controlled response

CORTEX

Metabolic and hormonal response

MID BRAIN

Postural reflexes

Automatic survival functions

BRAIN STEM

Primitive reflexes inhibited

SENSORY INPUT

39

It is through the process of primitive reflex inhibition and then postural reflex development, that the infant recapitulates evolution. The stages of his brain growth and the movements he makes are inextricably linked. Continuous brain development is facilitated through these movement sequences which lay down efficient neural pathways. *"Practice and repetition of movement patterns result in them being absorbed into the individual's repertoire of skills, probably also resulting in physical changes taking place in the neurons concerned, so that the flow of impulses along a specific pathway is facilitated. Repetition enhances facilitation and adeptness."* (Draper, 1993)

Chapter 4

THE SENSES

Long before a child ever reaches school age, he has begun to learn. His learning began at his conception and should continue to grow in unison with his body throughout his natural life. All learning takes place in the brain, but it is the body which acts as the vehicle by which knowledge is acquired. Both brain and body work together through the central nervous system (CNS), but both are dependent upon the senses for all information about the outer world.

When a child reaches school age it is generally assumed that the basic systems necessary for academic learning are established, and that good teaching, combined with the child's willingness to learn, will enable him to succeed. In order for him to be able to do this, at least three basic systems have to operate effectively:
1. The reception of information via the senses.
2. The processing of information in the brain.
3. Response or expression to that information via the efferent system.

Afferent system— information to the brain.

Efferent system— information from the brain to the body.

We have seen how the reflex system can affect performance at the levels of processing and response, causing brain stem reactions to direct the response without higher brain level involvement. Equally, distorted sensory input may awaken anew reflex activity which would otherwise be inhibited, and thus a vicious circle of distorted sensation and inappropriate response is established.

It has long been accepted that defects in vision and in hearing will impede the learning process, but they are generally investigated in isolation by an expert in each field. Frequently the child is only examined for deficit in one area and further investigations into what a child sees, what he hears or how he experiences touch, are not carried out. **Visual and auditory hypersensitivity are just as much of a handicap to learning as loss in these areas, and in some cases both hyper and hypo can coexist in a child.** (Delacato, 1974) Both vision and hearing are dependent upon the vestibular apparatus for their functioning, but the occupational therapist, and the audiologist work in separate departments and may never know that they both see the same child—one whose main problem is located in the inner ear.

Hyper — oversensitive, inadequate filtering of extraneous sensation

Hypo — undersensitive, inadequate sensations received

White sound— continuous background sensation, which is always present and intrudes upon other sensations.

41

When the system is overloaded, the child can go into a "shock" reaction. i.e. the sympathetic nervous system shuts down all sensation and ceases to respond to the stimulus. This may be interpreted as being under-sensitive, when in fact it is an extreme reaction to being oversensitive.

The sympathetic nervous system consists of a network of nerve fibers which—under stress ready the body for either flight or standing to fight. It does so by increasing the heartbeat, quickening breathing and enhancing the supply of oxygen to the muscles by siphoning the blood supply from the skin to the deep muscles.

Hence the pallor or the redness of the skin is a clue to the condition of the child.

The parasympathetic nervous system—its opposite partner in the balancing, self-regulating autonomic nervous system—increases salivary gland secretions, decreases the heart rate, promotes digestion and dilates the blood vessels.

None of the senses develop or operate in isolation. Each one is reinforced, modified and influenced by information from the others. Our language and our interpretation accepts cross-sensory reference as being fundamental to our understanding of the world: Hearing has been described as a "specialized sense of touch", we "taste with our nose", "feast with our eyes", "see with our fingers" and according to Tomatis we "read with our ears". We accept balance between the different aspects of our lives as being fundamental to health and to well-being, and yet "the sense of balance" is perhaps the forgotten sixth sense of the twentieth century. An understanding of the senses and how they complement one another is essential, if we are to understand and to help the child who cannot "make sense" of the world and therefore has difficulty learning through the accepted channels of education.

1. BALANCE AND THE VESTIBULAR SYSTEM

Balance is the core of functioning. It is the first system to be fully developed, becoming operational at 16 weeks in utero and is myelinated at birth, providing the fetus with a sense of direction and orientation inside the womb. It is in place to help cope with the problem of gravity, which the child will encounter in its full force for the first time when he is born.

The balance mechanism monitors all sensation in both directions between the brain and the body.

Every living creature shares one relationship: a relationship with gravity. It is gravity which provides us with our center, whether it be in space, in time, motion, depth or sense of self, acting as the nucleus from which all operations become possible. Problems in the balance system will have repercussions for all other areas of functioning. Such problems affect the sensory systems, because all sensation passes through the vestibular mechanism at brain stem level before being transmitted elsewhere for analysis.

The vestibular system operates closely with the reflexes to facilitate balance. It is located in the inner ear, and its job is to monitor and make adjustments to any movement of the head or the environment. *"As we move and interact with gravity, sensory receptors in the ear are activated, and impulses appraising the central nervous system about the position of the head in space are directed to various parts of the brain and down the spinal cord. It is believed that sensory impulses from the eyes, ears, muscles and joints must be matched to the vestibular input before such information can be reprocessed efficiently. If that is true, what we see, hear and feel makes sense only if the vestibular system is functioning adequately."* (Pyfer, J. & Johnson, R., 1981)

The Vestibular System has two main parts:

1.   Three fluid filled semicircular canals, set at right angles to each other.

2.   Two vestibular sacs, also filled with fluid.

Hair cells line the inside of both organs. Any movement of the body, particularly the head, sets up motion of the fluid in the canals and the sacs, stimulating the hair cells. Movement of the hair cells triggers the release of nerve signals which provide the brain with information about direction, angle and extent of the movement, so that appropriate muscle adjustments may be made. Certain hair cells are particularly sensitive to gravity, informing the brain of any deviation from the upright position. Signals from the vestibular system then pass along the vestibular nerve to the cerebellum. The cerebellum has been called "the moderator between sensation and brain level response" (Levinson, 1981) as it coordinates information from the inner ear with other parts of the body. It monitors where we are in space and what position we are in, i.e. standing, sitting, running, climbing, somersaulting, etc. If information from the vestibular system is out of alignment with information from the other senses, motion sickness results. Astronauts experience a unique form of this when placed in a gravity-free environment where their sense of "center" is lost, and they rely heavily on tactile and visual stimuli to retain a sense of location.

It has long been recognized that sensory deprivation will result in emotional and physical distress. In extreme cases it has been used as a method of interrogation and torture resulting in irreversible insanity within a very short period of time. The unfortunate victim was blindfolded, placed in a suit which covered him from head to toe (depriving him of external tactile stimuli) and "white sound" was played into the ears through a headset. If this did not yield results, the victim was then placed in a centrifuge and spun for several minutes with devastating effect. Very few victims ever recovered their sanity.

The vestibular is possibly the oldest and the most primitive of the sensory systems. It is believed that the human ear is an outgrowth or development of specific skin folds located around the gills of fish. The fish then rely upon the movement of the hairs situated in these sensitive areas to warn them of approaching obstacles, food and predators. In mammals the ear has become more highly developed, dividing into two structures:

1.   The vestibular apparatus or balance mechanism.
2.   The cochlear or auditory apparatus.

Frequently, they are viewed by specialists as separate systems, whereas in fact they share a common chamber, fluid, and transmission of information via the same cranial nerve, the VIIIth cranial nerve. Thus, hearing is bound to be influenced by information passing through the vestibular, and the vestibular is bound to be influenced by sound.

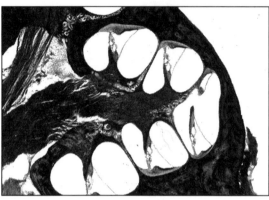

Left : Photo of a cochlea; Right: organ of Corti © 1995 Carolina Biological through Peter Arnold, Inc., New York, NY.

(See also illustrations on pages 52-53)

Hz:-
number of vibrations per second

Madaule (1993) stated that it is the vestibular portion alone which monitors slow movement, but that we also use the auditory component for movement which is traveling faster than a speed of 20Hz, using it to measure the distance between the two ears to locate where movement has occurred.

Steinbach (1994) suggests that "sound is not sound" but is the physical expression of movement or vibration. The ear then acts as a receptor and transmitter of vibration to be interpreted by the brain. Defects in the vestibular apparatus may affect the point at which the auditory system takes over, and problems in the auditory apparatus may result in the vestibular system working overtime to compensate.

Both the vestibular system and the reflex system are closely aligned to the visual system, acting as the substrata upon which oculo-motor and visual-perceptual skills are built. Impulses from the vestibular system to the brain stem affect equilibrium reactions, with motor nerves that control eye-movements and with nerves that lead to the somatosensory portion of the cerebral cortex.

"Vestibular input is necessary for static and dynamic balance development, eye-tracking ability and motor planning. Children who are slow to develop good vestibular functioning are delayed in all gross motor patterns which require coordination of both sides of the body. They may have difficulty in maintaining posture, with eye-hand coordination, and with fine motor control." (Pyfer, 1981) Inappropriate vestibular signals may elicit primitive reflex reactions, but equally,

44

aberrant reflex activity will impede the activities of the vestibular system. If a child is to utilize the information provided for him by his senses, there must be a balance between them.

****

Symptoms suggestive of vestibular dysfunction.
1. **Poor balance**
2. **Motion sickness**
3. **Dislike of heights, swings, carousels**
4. **Child is easily disoriented**
5. **Difficulty remaining still**
6. **Oculo-motor dysfunction**
7. **Visual perceptual difficulties**
8. **Poor directional awareness**
9. **Difficulties in space perception**
10. **Poor organizational skills—"dizzy" behavior, literally meaning "scatterbrained."**

****

TACTILITY

Although the vestibular system is the first to be fully developed and myelinated, it is the sense of touch which provides us with our first source of contact with the outer world. The first observed response to tactile stimulation occurs at approximately 5 weeks after conception with the emergence of the mass cutaneous withdrawal reflexes mentioned in Chapter 1. Gentle stimulation of the upper lip results in immediate withdrawal from the source of contact by the whole organism. The area of sensitivity rapidly spreads over the next 4 weeks to encompass the oral region of the face, the palms of the hands and the soles of the feet, until eventually the whole body surface is responsive to touch. However, the earliest primitive realization of touch is a defensive one characterized by withdrawal.

During the second and third trimesters of pregnancy tactile awareness should mature to allow the grasping reflexes to develop (palmar, plantar, rooting, suck, Moro, etc.), so that by the time the baby is born, touch is associated with security, with feeding, comfort and eventually exploration. Touch precedes both hearing and vision as the primary channel of learning: Touch receptors cover the entire body.

The area in the brain which perceives touch stretches like a headband and is called the somatosensory cortex. It is capable of registering heat, cold, pressure, pain and body position. The most sensitive areas of the body have a correspondingly large representation area in the somatosensory cortex, with the lips, hands and genital regions occupying a large section of the somatosensory map. Even the base of the hair follicles have touch receptors. Just as fish register movement through the motion of hairs on the skin surface and the vestibular apparatus functions through the movement of fluid over hair cells, the sense of touch is essential for the functioning of balance, orientation and motion.

Dermis—
top layer of the skin.

Ayres (1980) divided the tactile system into protective and discriminative subsystems: Protective receptors are located around the hair follicles and respond to subtle stimulation such as sound and air waves (vibration) moving across the body. *"They literally tell us where our body ends and where space begins."* (Pyfer, 1981). Discriminative receptors are located in the dermis and respond when we come into contact with something—either actively or passively. These systems should be mutually exclusive, that is: one shuts down as the other comes into action. The protective system stays in operation until we are touched, and unless that contact is threatening, the discriminative system comes into play as soon as contact takes place.

The child who has an over-active protective system will be "tactile defensive" and may still have uninhibited cutaneous withdrawal reflexes which continue to influence the central nervous system. If this is the case, then touch can be neither an instant source of comfort nor a purveyor of information, for the reflex response will elicit withdrawal from the source of contact, and the child cannot adequately utilize his tactile discrimination skills. The "hyper-tactile" child may have abnormal perception in all input to the area of the cortex which registers touch. He may have poor tolerance and/or adaptive mechanisms to heat and cold. He may have a low pain threshold, particularly to pain associated with piercing the skin, but, paradoxically, a high tolerance to internal pain.

This may be the child who over-reacts to injections, grazes and small cuts, but who will fail to notice that his legs are covered with bruises. He may dislike any form of physical contact and therefore have difficulty in either receiving or demonstrating affection, which makes it difficult for the mother to establish a warm relationship with the child. He may appear to be inordinately stubborn about the clothes he wears and the way that he does things. Contact sports may be avoided, and the child may have a poor body image and sense of his own space.

In extreme, this may play a significant part in the distortion of body image, which is characteristic of anorexia nervosa. The anorexic "feels" herself to be fat and believes her own body space to occupy a far greater area than it actually does. Despite all attempts to shrink from within, no amount of weight loss will alter this sensation, as proportionally the same amount of skin surface and therefore number of receptors remain in contact with the outer world. Because sensation of this type is mediated at the brain stem, the feeling will over-ride any logic that is imposed from the cortex, and no amount of evidence to the contrary will change the anorexic's perception of herself.

Tactile discrimination should provide us with an enormous amount of information about our environment. Studies with rats have shown that offspring handled in the laboratory have better immune systems and gain weight better. Early handling also leads to permanent sensitivity of the part of the brain that controls the stress response, resulting in reduced levels of stress hormones. Without touch, small children rapidly become disturbed and may attempt to supply themselves with essential sensory information by self-stimulation. One example of this is the institutionalized "rocking" observed amongst so many children abandoned in orphanages. Too often it is assumed to be a sign of mental retardation instead of being regarded as an attempt by the child to provide himself with essential vestibular, tactile and proprioceptive information. Studies of premature infants have shown a 45% increase in weight gain amongst children who are massaged for 15 minutes, 3 times a day.

In the early months of life, it is the mouth—through rooting, sucking and exploring with the lips and tongue—which provides the neonate and the infant with its primary source of tactile information. The hands are also involved—initially in palmar movements and Babkin response—and then later, in an interplay between hand and mouth. This is the so-called "oral" phase of development. As in the growth of prenatal tactile response, postnatal tactile development starts with the mouth and spreads outward to the hands, the feet and eventually the entire body. If either tactile withdrawal or grasp reflexes remain prevalent beyond their allotted time, they will disrupt the delicate balance between the protective and the discriminative tactile systems.

Babkin response during nursing: palming movements in the hands causing pursing of the lips. Sucking movements may result in kneading motions of the hands—kittens also do this when being fed.

As children grow older, physical contact with the parents diminishes. At puberty the adolescent tentatively seeks tactile stimulation anew with the blossoming of sexual awareness, so that a cycle of search for contact continues through life. It is perhaps the 8-16 year-old age group who will suffer most if they have undetected tactile problems, for this is the age when the child must seek tactile information for himself—parents and teachers no longer supply it with the richness that they did during infancy. The child who lacks sufficient protective control will be the dare-devil, who does not sense danger, is frequently oblivious to injury either to himself or to others, and who cannot read other people's body language. He presents a danger to himself and everyone around him—he is literally "thick-skinned", unlike his tactile defensive counterpart who will shy away from activities and experiences for which he is inadequately equipped.

****

Symptoms of hypertactility.

1 **Hypersensitivity**
2. **Dislike of being touched, but may be a compulsive "toucher"**
3. **Allergic skin reactions**
4. **Poor temperature control**
5. **Low external pain threshold**
6. **Anorexia**
7. **Dislike of sports**
8. **Tendency to rely on sensory instead of verbal language**

****

****

Symptoms of hypotactility.

1. **Hypotactile**
2. **High threshold of pain**
3. **Craving for contact sports**
4. **Child may provoke roughhousing or fighting**
5. **Compulsive touching**
6. **"Bull in a china shop"**

****

AUDITORY

Fig. 13 — © 1995 through Peter Arnold, Inc., New York, NY.

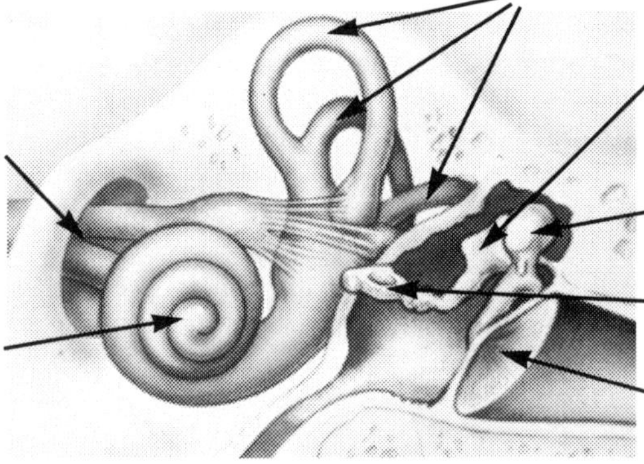

Semicircular canals

Hammer (Malleus)

Nerves to brain

Anvil (Incus)

Stirrup (Stapes)

Cochlea

Eardrum (Typanum)

Hearing, like vestibular sensation and touch, is the reception and transmission of energy through motion and vibration. The human ear is a compound development, forming during the second half of the embryonic period (4-8 weeks in utero). As the ossicles of the middle ear develop, central nervous system connections are established to the cochlear and the vestibular structures. Myelination of auditory fibers occurs between the 24th and the 28th week in utero, and sound perception develops slowly from this time onward. At this stage, the ear is tuned specifically to the sounds heard in utero, but the fetus will respond to some external auditory stimuli as well.

For the first few days after birth the ears are still filled with superfluous fluid, (similar to the water in the ears after swimming or bathing) with the result that the infant inhabits an auditory no-man's-land between uterine and extra-uterine sound. Once the fluid has cleared, the neonate ears become receptive to a vast range of sound frequencies, something in the region of 0-20,000 Hertz and beyond.

The number of vibrations will determine the pitch of the sound heard. e.g. 125 Hz is low sound, 8000 Hz is perceived as high sound.

During the first 3 years of life, the child must learn to use his ears to "tune-in" to the specific frequencies of his own language, in much the same way that a radio is adjusted to select specific stations. It is at this time that the child has the potential to learn any language if it is exposed to the sounds of that language continuously over a period of time, no matter what language his mother speaks. After the age of 3 years, when these fine tuning adjustments should have been made, it becomes far more difficult to assimilate a new language.

Hearing **loss** has long been recognized as being an enormous handicap linguistically, educationally and socially. Much less attention has been paid until recently to problems of hearing **discrimination** amongst children with learning difficulties or with language disorders. Speech may have developed at the correct time but the more detailed analysis of sounds essential for reading and spelling may have been omitted: The child cannot hear the difference between similar or blended sounds such as "ch" and "sh", "th" and "f", "p" and "b". If the letters sound the same to him, he presumes that they should be spelled the same way. Storr (1993) discusses two essential components for reading—vision and hearing. He talks about the "auditory reader" who is not just a phonetic reader, but who reads silently with an "inner voice" which enables him to see and hear the words inside his head, as if they were being read out loud. Poor auditory discrimination skills will impede this process.

Frequent ear, nose and throat infections in early childhood resulting in intermittent hearing loss over a period of time can prevent the development of such auditory discrimination skills. Lack of auditory stimulation, or even a constant cacophony of background noise in early life can discourage early "listening" and the child may learn to shut out and ignore sound from an early age.

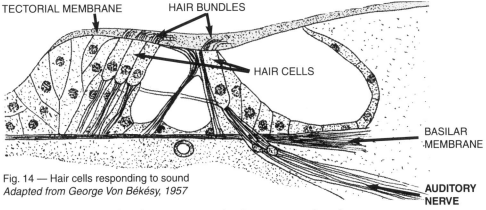

Fig. 14 — Hair cells responding to sound
Adapted from George Von Békésy, 1957

Scientists in New York using a superconducting quantum interference device (SQID), which senses tiny changes in magnetic fields on a brain listening to music, have found an eerie reflection of the black and white keys of a piano responding in the brain to the notes that were heard. *"The brain hears loud sounds in a totally different place from quieter sounds, but the areas which register tones are laid out like a keyboard."* (Williamson, 1992). It is possible that failure to register specific sounds at the crucial stage for language learning may result in part of the keyboard or sound map being omitted or ceasing to respond.

Hearing too much or "auditory hypersensitivity" can be just as much of a problem as hearing deficit. The inability to filter or occlude miscellaneous sound, suggests poorly developed listening skills, and can have profound effect upon later learning, language, communication, and behavior. In the last 20 years research has turned to focus upon the problems of "listening", as opposed to problems of hearing. Tomatis, in France, and Christian Volf, in Denmark, quite independently of each other, were pioneers in this approach. Since then, various techniques have been devised to assess and to retrain the listening skills of individuals with such diverse problems as autism, hyperactivity, dyslexia, depression and imperfect pitch discrimination amongst musicians.

Tomatis has shown that there is a difference in the way that sounds are transmitted to the language processing center in the brain, depending on which ear is used as the dominant listening ear. The right ear is the most efficient of the two for receiving and transmitting sounds of language, and left-eared children may be at a disadvantage. Sounds heard through the right ear pass directly to the main language center in the left hemisphere (Fig. 15a). Sounds heard via the left ear pass first to the sub-language center in the right hemisphere and then have to pass through the corpus callosum to the left hemisphere for decoding (Fig.15b). There is a delay in milliseconds, similar to the delay experienced on an overseas telephone call, while the sounds pass to the satellite and down again. The child who is primarily left-eared may have difficulty in following a list of verbal instructions as he is still decoding the first two instructions when the third is being given.

Lack of ear preference may further confuse the situation, resulting in sounds reaching the brain in a different order from the order they are arranged phonetically in a word, i.e. the child who switches ear preference while listening or sounding out a word may find the sounds processed through the left ear arrive a fraction later than the sounds processed through the right ear, irrespective of their correct order. For example, if the word phon/et/ic was heard, using the left ear for the first syllable and the right ear for the latter two, it may arrive at the brain as "eticphon" or even "etphonic". Inconsistencies in spelling involving letter, syllable and word reversals are a logical outcome.

Fig. 15a   Fig. 15b

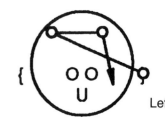

Right   Left   Right   Left

Speech Center   Speech Center

If the child is to be able to hear words and then to separate specific sounds and distinguish the phonemes and formants in them, he needs to have excellent hearing throughout the range of frequencies from 125 Hz to 8000 Hz. Every language has its unique frequency band, within which fall all the sounds used in that language. Key stages or windows for learning are well known, and if that key stage is missed, the chances of subsequently developing skills in that area are considerably reduced. The "window" for language is during the first three years of life—exactly the same time that the ears should be making their fine tuning adjustments. The child learns to filter out unnecessary sounds, and tune in to the sounds of language, so that he can start to hear and to reproduce the sounds necessary for speech and later for written language.

dB — decibels: measure of volume of sound

A volume of 20dB is considered normal. A volume of 40dB would be considered adequate but not ideal for a child to cope in a noisy classroom by most school doctors or audiologists whose primary job is to detect hearing deficit. A child whose hearing falls between 20 and 40dB will not therefore be considered sufficiently severe to warrant treatment. Nevertheless, this type of hearing can have profound effects upon the child's ability to discriminate between similar but different sounds such as "sh" and "ch", "f" and "th," etc. 40-60dB would be considered moderate hearing loss, 60dB and beyond severe hearing loss.

20dB is approximately the volume of a quiet telephone conversation

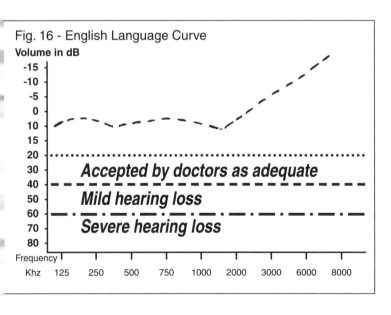

As the chart demonstrates, however, the English language curve requires discrimination at levels far more sensitive than 20dB, particularly in the high frequencies which are involved in sounds such as f, s, sh, ch, th, etc. Vowel and consonant sounds cross the spectrum of frequencies so that minor deviations from the language curve may cause specific speech and spelling problems.

51

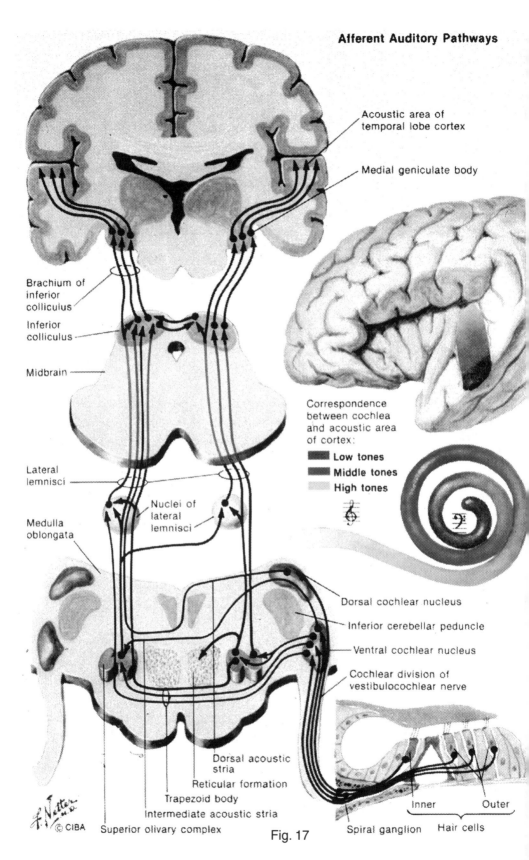

Afferent Auditory Pathways

Acoustic area of temporal lobe cortex

Medial geniculate body

Brachium of inferior colliculus

Inferior colliculus

Midbrain

Lateral lemnisci

Nuclei of lateral lemnisci

Medulla oblongata

Correspondence between cochlea and acoustic area of cortex:

Low tones
Middle tones
High tones

Dorsal cochlear nucleus

Inferior cerebellar peduncle

Ventral cochlear nucleus

Cochlear division of vestibulocochlear nerve

Dorsal acoustic stria

Reticular formation

Trapezoid body

Intermediate acoustic stria

Superior olivary complex

Spiral ganglion

Inner   Outer

Hair cells

Fig. 17

52

Figures on page 52 and page 53 © copyright 1953. CIBA-GEIGY Corp. Reprinted with permission from The Ciba Collection of Medical Illustrations, Vol. 1, illustrated by Frank H. Netter, M.D. All rights reserved.

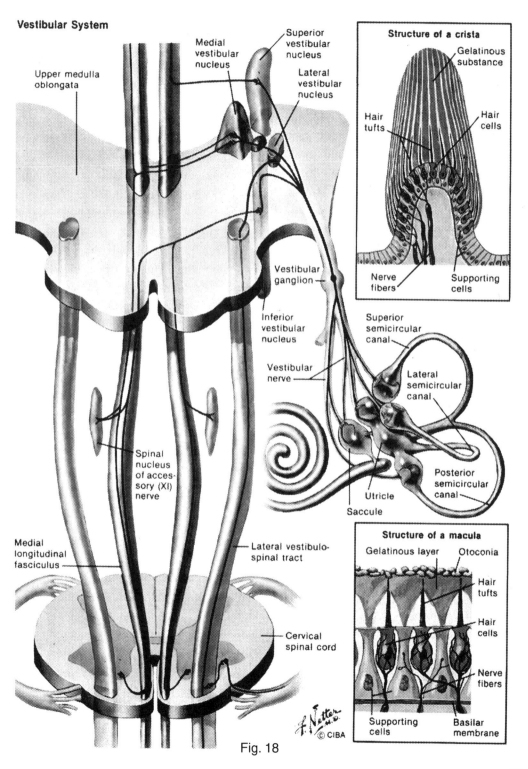

Vestibular System

Upper medulla oblongata

Medial vestibular nucleus

Superior vestibular nucleus

Lateral vestibular nucleus

Structure of a crista

Gelatinous substance

Hair tufts

Hair cells

Nerve fibers

Supporting cells

Vestibular ganglion

Inferior vestibular nucleus

Vestibular nerve

Superior semicircular canal

Lateral semicircular canal

Posterior semicircular canal

Utricle

Saccule

Spinal nucleus of accessory (XI) nerve

Medial longitudinal fasciculus

Lateral vestibulo-spinal tract

Cervical spinal cord

Structure of a macula

Gelatinous layer

Otoconia

Hair tufts

Hair cells

Nerve fibers

Supporting cells

Basilar membrane

F. Netter M.D. © CIBA

Fig. 18

53

Some children suffer from hyperacuity, but as this is not measured in standard hearing tests, the child is again dismissed as not having a problem. Hearing too much can result in enormous concentration difficulties, speech difficulties and problems with social interaction. Tomatis described how high frequency sound is "energizing" while low frequency sound tends to be relaxing or "enervating". Clinical tests on a number of hyperactive children at The Institute for Neuro-Physiological Psychology have revealed them to be hypersensitive in the <u>high</u> frequency range of sounds, in some cases still perceiving sounds between 2000 and 6000 Hz at a volume of (minus) -10 dB and beyond. One boy was even convinced he had extra-sensory perception as he knew a car was coming round a corner several minutes before anyone else. He was very upset when it was suggested to him that he did have "super" sensory perception, but only because his hearing was so acute!

Dr. Kjeld Johansen, at the Dyslexia Research Laboratory in Gudhjem, Denmark, has devised a system of assessing and treating problems of auditory discrimination and auditory processing. Over 20 years of independent research developed from the original ideas of Christian Volf have resulted in a therapeutic approach which has been statistically proven to be effective. Audiometric tests are carried out to measure monaural thresholds and to determine hearing acuity throughout the hearing range. A dichotic listening test is also used to establish which is the primary leading ear. Once the tests have been analyzed, the child is given an audio tape to listen to for 10 minutes per day. Specific tapes have been made in which all sounds except the frequencies the child has difficulty hearing have been filtered out. By listening to pure frequencies unpolluted by extraneous sound, the child can start to "hear" the sounds that it was formerly unable to discriminate. The tapes are also specially adjusted to encourage right eared listening. The tapes are altered at 6-8 weekly intervals, and hearing rechecked every few months to insure that improvements are occurring. As the child's listening skills improve, concomitant changes take place in reading, writing, use of language and behavior.

The value of music for learning has long been recognized, but with financial cut backs and changes in methods of education, music has taken a back seat in the early learning years of many children. Vast improvements have been made in electronic sound equipment. Because it is so inexpensive and easily available, a lot of music is now heard through tapes, discs or synthesizers where many of the beneficial high frequency sounds are lost.

Live music—sadly—is today a rare experience for many children. Previous generations of children learned multiplication tables, alphabet and Latin verbs to tunes. Understanding of what they had learned came later, but the tune and the rhythm aided recall. Most people can still remember the words to all the verses of any hymn if someone sings the first few notes of the tune for them. Without the music, they cannot find the words. The Master of Choristers at an English cathedral said that the reading age of all his choir boys improved by 12 months within 6 months of their joining the choir. This remained true irrespective of whether they were good or poor readers at the time of joining. It could be said that this was the direct result of the amount of written material they had to sing, but it could also be said that the dual processes of listening, vocalizing, and learning to hear pitch and rhythm enhanced other skills. Dr. Audrey Wisbey, in Cambridge, found much the same reading improvement. Cathedrals and other large old public buildings have acoustics which are rich in the high frequencies, which are lost in the low ceiling, carpeted and cushioned buildings of our time.

"Sound is not sound." (Steinbach, 1994) Sound is vibration, motion and energy. If we hear no sound we perceive danger, for the totally silent world is a dead world. Sound passes through all levels of the brain, affecting not just the ear and the vestibular but also our bodies through bone conduction. The significance of sound for learning is immeasurable.

****
Symptoms of auditory problems.

1. **Short attention span**
2. **Distractibility**
3. **Hypersensitivity to sounds**
4. **Misinterpretation of questions**
5. **Confusion of similar sounding words, frequent need to have a word repeated.**
6. **Inability to follow sequential instructions**
7. **Flat and monotonous voice**
8. **Hesitant speech**
9. **Weak vocabulary**
10. **Poor sentence structure**
11. **Inability to sing in tune**
12. **Confusion or reversal of letters**
13. **Poor reading comprehension**
14. **Poor reading aloud**
15. **Poor spelling**
16. **Auditory delay**

****

VISUAL

Vision is obviously essential for academic learning. The skills of reading, writing, spelling and arithmetic are all dependent upon the ability to see written symbols. When learning difficulties arise, vision is often the first area to be checked. If the child passes a simple eye test which only assesses distance vision, further investigation into visual problems are seldom pursued. Distance vision is only one component in the complex sense of sight. How we see, the way that we use our eyes and how we perceive the world through sight, is the result of a complex series of connections and neural developments which should have taken place in the early formative years, and which are dependent upon adequate maturation of the central nervous system. (CNS)

First of all, both eyes must work as a team so that each eye is directed to the same fixation point on the page, rather like two spotlights highlighting a dancer on the center of the stage.

Left
eye

Right
eye

This is called convergence and must be fully developed for the eyes to scan along a line of letters and send a clear single image to the brain. Fig. 19 shows the drawings of one 13 year old boy whose eyes never learned to converge, so that he still sees two separate images on the paper. It is not surprising that he has enormous difficulties with all written material.

Fig. 19

A second necessity is that the image seen by each eye must be sharp, clearly focused. The focus must be adjusted quickly from one distance or one angle to another. This skill is called <u>accommodation</u>. Difficulties with either accommodation or convergence can affect one another.

After that, in order to read easily, it is necessary to be able to scan or track along a line of print smoothly and evenly, so that the brain can receive a flow of sequentially correct information. Tracking is vital for orderly progression from one word to another, or finding the way from line to line without loss of place. In addition to the three skills of convergence, accommodation and tracking, a child also needs to have good directional awareness to distinguish similar but directionally different symbols such as p/q, b/d, on/no, left/felt, etc. (Duighan, 1994)

Directional awareness is a vestibular based skill. The vestibular system acts like an internal compass to give us a sense of "center" from which we can automatically judge up from down, left from right, start from finish. The development of cerebral dominance at the age of 7-8 years cements this knowledge, but the problems with direction may still persist after cerebral dominance has occurred if vestibular functioning is faulty. This may be the child who gets easily lost in new surroundings, has difficulty learning to tell time on an old fashioned clock and who has poor organizational skills.

Reading difficulty is only the tip of the iceberg where visual problems are concerned. Handwriting and spelling will also be profoundly affected, as is coordination, because the child will have poor spatial awareness, poor body image and impaired hand-eye coordination. Many sports and leisure activities will only be performed with great effort, and levels of attainment will be disproportionate to the energy and enthusiasm initially applied to the task. The child will become frustrated, and may soon start to avoid activities enjoyed by other children and thus unwittingly increase his own sense of isolation. It has been suggested (Trevor-Roper, 1990) that visual difficulties directly influence the choice of subjects, hobbies and eventually the career that an individual will make.

Trevor-Roper cites the myopic child as the child who rarely becomes a good sportsman, and who concentrates upon artistic or "bookish" pastimes, which fall directly within his field of nearpoint vision. He links developments in the Impressionist school of painting to the corresponding deterioration in the artists' eyesight during the later years of their lives, when clarity of form in their paintings increasingly gave way to the representation of the interplay of light forms.

Myopic —
short sighted: good
near-distance vision,
poor distance vision
beyond 12 to 24
inches.

Since poor visual information will impair the recognition and recall of groups of letters either as units or as a picture (visio-spatial awareness), spelling will be affected. Visual imagery or visualization is necessary for spelling, as it enables the child to form templates or a visual memory for words in the mind's eye. These are then matched against the written word to assess whether the word "looks" right, i.e. is there a variable within the word which does not correspond to the remembered visual image of that word? As our hearing deteriorates gradually over the years, we use auditory memory to continue to speak and to pronounce words correctly. So, also do we need a visual memory to be able to write and to spell words accurately.

The effect of aberrant reflex activity upon oculomotor functioning was discussed in Chapter 1, with the asymmetrical tonic neck reflex (ATNR) having an adverse effect upon tracking, the tonic labyrinthine reflex (TLR) upon convergence, the Moro reflex upon fixation and the symmetrical tonic neck reflex STNR upon the readjustment of binocular vision from one distance to another.

Dysfunction in these areas will inevitably result in visual-perceptual difficulties. It is important that an examination be carried out to assess what a child sees and to investigate the way his eyes work together. On the next page are two examples of severe visual-perceptual difficulties. Both children were in a normal school struggling to keep up with academic work. They were asked to copy the Tansley Standard Figures and the Bender Visual Gestalt Figures.

Despite a history of reading, writing and spelling difficulties, the visual-perceptual and visual-motor integration skills of these children had not previously been investigated. Child A and Child B also had a cluster of aberrant primitive reflexes.

Fig. 20 —
Bender-Gestalt test

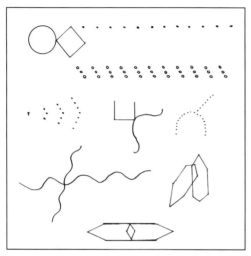

Child A — First test on left, second test after 5 months therapy on right

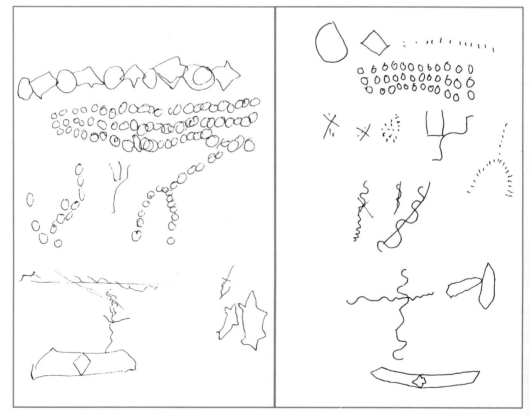

Fig. 21 —
Tansley Standard Visual Figures test

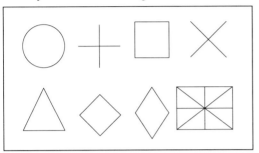

A.E. Tansley 1967

Child B — First test (top figure), second test (bottom figure) after 3 months therapy.

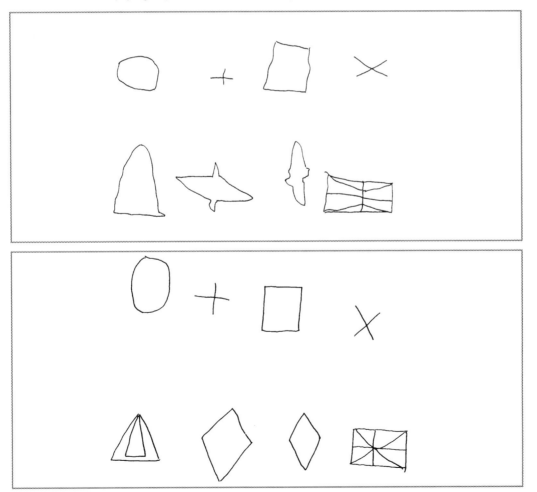

It must be remembered that the eye is only an instrument of vision. To make effective use of the sights eyes provide, the child must also make use of other sensory information. The foundations for these interconnections are laid down during the first year of life, at the time that neural pathways are formed between the eye, the brain and the body. Vision is particularly dependent upon one of these pathways: the Vestibulo Ocular Reflex Arc (VOR).

Fig. 22

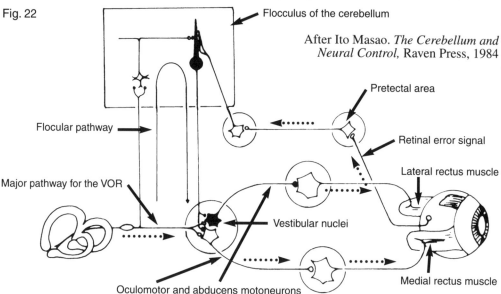

Flocculus of the cerebellum

After Ito Masao. *The Cerebellum and Neural Control*, Raven Press, 1984

Pretectal area

Flocular pathway

Retinal error signal

Lateral rectus muscle

Major pathway for the VOR

Vestibular nuclei

Medial rectus muscle

Oculomotor and abducens motoneurons

Interaction between the components of this loop will determine the efficiency of the visual system in later life: i.e. the rapid exchange of information between the vestibular apparatus, the eyes, and the level of reflex response to incoming stimuli. Any defect in one of these elements will affect the smooth operation of the whole.

****
Symptoms indicative of visual stress:
1. **Misreading words**
2. **Missing or repeating words or lines**
3. **Slow reading**
4. **Need to use finger or marker as a pointer**
5. **Inability to remember what has been read**
6. **Fatigue after reading or writing**
7. **Poor concentration**
8. **Child describes letters which "move", "jump" or are poorly focused**
9. **Reading at a very close distance**
10. **Reading with one eye covered or sideways posture**
11. **Distractibility (stimulus bound effect)**
12. **Poor posture when reading or writing**
13. **Poorly spaced work**
14. **Handwriting crooked, or slopes in different directions, letters poorly balanced**
15. **Clumsiness**
16. **Difficulty with ball games.**

****

PROPRIOCEPTION

Closely allied to the other senses and interdependent upon them is the compound sense of proprioception. While it is the result of multisensory information, it also forms an information channel of its own. Proprioception or kinesthesis enables us to know where parts of our body are at any time, and to make the appropriate postural adjustments. It is an internal sense of physical self which allows us to carry out detailed maneuvers without conscious awareness and in the absence of other sensory cues.

Proprioceptors are located throughout the body in the joints, tendons, muscles, etc. Their input is processed primarily through the vestibular system, but also coordinates with information from all other sensory sources to influence body movements and direct adjustments for fine muscle coordination. Needless to say, distorted information coming from any one of these sources will also affect proprioception.

While proprioception and kinethethis are often used interchangeably, the term proprioception encompasses all sensations involving body position, either at rest or in motion, the term kinesthesia refers only to sensations arising when active muscle contraction becomes involved. Thus, some children who have little proprioceptive input when they sit still, may constantly have to move because they rely on information from the muscle movement on where they are in space.

In such a case, visual skills should also be checked.

Poor proprioceptive awareness is common among children with learning difficulties. Paradoxically, a small number will rely too heavily upon either proprioception or kinesthesis to perform certain tasks. For example: A 7 year old boy was asked to throw a bean bag into a box of sand from a distance of ten feet. The first four attempts missed the target, but on the fifth, the bag dropped into the box. Each subsequent throw was successful, until the box was moved one foot closer to him. Theoretically, this should have been easier, but he overshot the target at the next five throws. Thomas had poor depth perception and was relying upon proprioceptive information to direct the force of his throw once he had been successful he knew the "feel" of the throw necessary to hit the target. The same "feel" could not be useful to him once the target was moved.

Many children with poor individual sensory perception will attempt to use proprioception instead of the primary channel for learning. It is rather like using a huge net in an attempt to catch one individual fish. Learning can only be consistently successful if eyes, ears and balance system are also providing accurate information about changing circumstances. The child who attempts to use proprioception to compensate for weakness in another channel may be the child for whom "practice makes perfect . . . <u>sometimes</u>" and who will, at times, produce excellent results but appears to be inconsistent in his performance.

The child who will trace the shape of a letter or figure with his finger may be the one who cannot "see" it clearly. This may result in the development of splinter skills. The child will make the teacher believe he can do something, but she does not realize he has acquired a skill which cannot help him when it comes to more sophisticated learning.

****

Symptoms of poor proprioception

1. **Poor posture**
2. **Constant fidgeting or moving**
3. **Excessive desire to be held**
4. **May provoke fights to get sensory input**
5. **May have visual problems**

****

TASTE AND SMELL

The significance of taste and smell for learning is perhaps largely concentrated in the earliest years of a child's life, when his mouth is his primary source of information, exploration, expression and satisfaction. What does it taste like? Is it soft? Can I chew it? How big is it? etc. All early discoveries are made through the mouth.

Much of taste is dependent upon the sense of smell, as we know only too well when we have a bad cold and can only taste the specific tongue tastes of salty, bitter, sweet, and sour. Smell is, perhaps, the most evocative of all the senses, instantaneously spanning decades in its ability to remind us of a certain place, person or event.

Instead of being routed through the thalamus—like the other sensory information—the nerves in the nasal passages send messages directly to the brain's olfactory bulbs which then spread the impulses to areas of the brain where memories are stored. Thus, a certain perfume will remind us of our mother when we were a small child and she was dressed up to go out for the evening, or the typical sounds and smells of a country we have visited. Smell can instantly summon multisensory images. It can also stimulate the production of hormones involved in the control of appetite, temperature and sexuality —the same region in the brain influenced by the Moro reflex: the hypothalamus.

> *The smell of school can easily become associated with stress, the smell of a hospital with pain.*

Taste and smell provide important information about an ever changing environment. Their significance to learning is hard to pinpoint, but as they evoke memories of past experiences, they enrich a child's understanding of what the teacher is trying to convey.

****

SYMPTOMS OF PROBLEMS WITH TASTE OR SMELL

HYPER

1. Child may avoid going to the bathroom because he cannot stand the smell of the antiseptics used, and is at risk of wetting his pants.
2. Child may avoid other children, especially those who come to school with dirty or smelly clothes.
3. Child may misbehave after floors have been polished.
4. Child may avoid eating in the cafeteria or be "faddy" about foods which have a strong smell.
5. Dislike of close proximity to other people.

HYPO

Child may eat indiscriminately, is at risk of eating substances labeled *Keep out of reach of children*.

****

SUMMARY

In some cases, sensory imbalance can be used to produce a rare streak of genius. For example, the accomplished musician who has highly sensitive and highly developed hearing in a specific range; the artist who is able to use slight visual distortion to create an image of the world that is truly unique; the writer, who is able to summon up emotion, experience and imaginations to give birth to a rich tapestry of characters and events; the actress who can literally feel herself into someone else's persona. These people have been able to gain insight from their particular sensory experience, and they have also had the skills which allowed them to turn this unusual ability to their advantage. The child who experiences failure from an early age on lacks the skill with which to profit from his own special window on the world. Our sensory receptors provide us with such an open window, through which we feel, perceive and maintain contact with the world around us.

Deprivation of even one of the senses will have a profound effect upon the individual, as will any alteration in the transmission of information via one of the sensory channels. <u>Mode</u>, <u>intensity</u> and <u>duration</u> of sensation are also of prime significance, as the type and degree of sensory input will directly influence the level of response that is given. Too little sensation may result in lack of response. Too much, may result in overreaction or vastly increased levels of stress as the individual attempts to maintain control over his response. Distortion or blurring of sensation, may result in confusion and inappropriate response.

Finally, there needs to be a balance between the different sensory channels so that cross-sensory reference may occur, in order to provide the individual with multi-sensory information about his environment, to which he may then adapt his responses. This is sensory integration.

When assessing a child with learning, language or behavioral difficulties, it is not sufficient to merely identify a hearing problem, a reading problem, a coordination problem, etc. It is necessary to look further and to ask, <u>What</u> does he hear? <u>How</u> does he see? <u>Under which specific situations</u> is his balance poor? Does he have the mature combination of movements necessary to read, to write and to speak? If a child does not see, hear or move in the way that it is assumed he should, the very foundations of learning are lacking.

Chapter 5

REFLEX TESTING

Tests listed:

1.   Moro Reflex Standard Test
2.   Moro Reflex Erect Test (Clarke, Bennett, and Rowston)
3.   Palmar Reflex
4.   Asymmetrical Tonic Neck Reflex Standard Test
5.   Asymmetrical Tonic Neck Reflex Schilder Test
6.   Rooting Reflex
7.   Suck Reflex
8.   Spinal Galant Reflex
9.   Tonic Labyrinthine Reflex Erect Test
10.   Symmetrical Tonic Neck Test
11.   Landau Reflex
12.   Amphibian Reflex Prone—Supine
13.   Segmental Rolling Reflex Hips Shoulders
14.   Oculo-Headrighting Reflexes
15.   Labyrinthine Headrighting Reflexes

The following test procedures relating to reflexes discussed in the text should be used for purposes of identification only, as they represent just one section of a complete diagnostic assessment for Neuro-Developmental Delay. Reflex inhibition training should only be undertaken after a full assessment and under the supervision of a qualified therapist.

****

SCORING
A scale of 0 4 is used:

0 = No abnormality detected, i.e. no evidence of
   a primitive reflex, or postural reflex fully developed
1 = evidence of primitive reflex to 25%
   partial absence of a postural reflex to 25%
2 = residual presence of a primitive reflex to 50%
   underdeveloped postural reflex to 50%
3 = virtually retained primitive reflex to 75%
   virtual absence of postural reflex to 75%
4 = retained primitive reflex, 100% present,
   complete absence of postural reflexes.

****

1. Moro Reflex
Standard Test for Vestibular-Activated Moro

Emergence: 9-32 weeks in utero
Birth: fully present
Inhibited: 2-4 months neonate

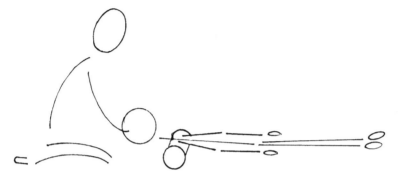

Test position
Supine, with arms flexed and hands resting on the floor. Shoulders should be raised with a small cushion and the child's head supported in the tester's hands and elevated approximately 2 inches above the level of the spine.

Test procedure
After just a few moments the tester should allow the child's head to drop 2-3 inches to just below the level of the spine, but not to reach the floor, having first given the instruction, "When you feel your head drop you must clasp your hands together across your chest as quickly as you can."

Observations
Any movement of the arms outward away from the body. Inability to bring the arms across the chest, or delayed action. Disorientation or distress as a result of the test procedure.

Scoring
0	immediate hand clasp and no adverse reaction
1	slight delay in reaction
2	delayed reaction, incomplete hand/arm movement or breath holding
3	no arm movement, alteration in breathing, and visible dislike of testing procedure
4	movement of the arms outward away from the body, leg extension and/or distress

Also note any reddening of skin or pallor immediately after testing

2. Moro Reflex
   Erect Test
   (Clarke, Bennett and Rowston)
   for
   Vestibular-activated Moro

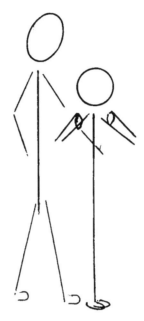

Test Position
Subject stands with feet together,
arms bent and held at 45° from the body
with the hands flexed at the wrists.

Test Procedure
Tester stands behind the subject and instructs the child to put his head
back as if looking at the ceiling and to close his eyes. Note any arm
movement or loss of balance as a result of putting the head into
extension. Once the subject has stabilized in this position, give the
instruction to remain still and fall backwards "like a soldier on parade"
at a given sound. Tester must be prepared to catch the full weight of the
subject.

Observations
Abduction of the arms on falling back and/or intake of breath or cry as
he loses the center of balance. Is there notable reddening of the skin or
pallor, tremor and "withdrawal" immediately after testing?

Scoring
0   subject falls back with no alteration of arm position
1   reddening of the skin or slight but quickly controlled
          movement of the arms or hands outwards
2   inability to drop back , movement of the arms and hands
          outwards, dislike of procedure
3   movement of the arms accompanied by "freezing"
          momentarily in this position, gasp of breath, reddening of the
          skin or pallor
4   complete abduction of the arms and hands outward
          accompanied by gasp, freeze and possible cry. Visible
          dislike or distress

3. Palmar reflex

Emergence: 11 weeks in utero
Birth: present
Inhibited: 2-3 months neonate

Test position
Standing, feet together with arms bent and palms upturned in a flexed, relaxed position, elbows away from the body.

Test procedure
Gently stroke with a soft brush along the creases of the palm. Repeat twice.

Observations
Any movement of the fingers or thumb inwards toward the stimulus, or extreme sensitivity in the palmar region.

Scoring
0	no response
1	slight movement of the fingers or thumb inward
2	definite movement of the thumb or fingers inward, subject complains touch is ticklish or painful
3	movement of the thumb and/or fingers inward as if to grasp the stimulus, rubbing of the hands immediately after testing
4	thumb and fingers close in on stimulation. This may be accompanied by simultaneous movements of the lips

4. Asymmetrical Tonic Neck Reflex Standard Test

(This test is designed to be used on young babies and may or may not elicit response in an older child who has developed musculature and methods of compensation and control)

Emergence: 18 weeks in utero
Birth: present
Inhibited: 4-6 months of life

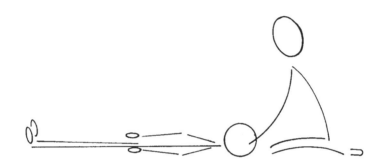

Test position
Supine with arms flexed away from the body and hands resting on finger tips.

Test procedure
Ensure the subject's head is relaxed at the midline. Slowly rotate the head to one side. Hold in that position for 15-20 seconds and observe reactions in arms and legs. Return the head to the midline. Pause for several seconds. Slowly rotate the head to the other side. Pause for 15- 20 seconds. Repeat procedure 3-4 times.

Observations
Note any movement in the body on the side to which the head is turned, particularly in the hand, arm, foot and leg on that side. Any tendency to increased extensor tone on the side to which the head is turned suggests an ATNR might be present. Inability to relax the neck muscles or permit turning of the head beyond a specific point may also suggest a controlled ATNR.

Scoring

0	no response
1	slight tremor in the fingers
2	movement of the hand, arm or leg, or alteration of muscle tone through the torso
3	involuntary extensor movement of any part of the body on the side to which the head is turned, or flexion of the side
4	full extension of the arm and/or leg on the side to which the head is turned with flexion of occipital limbs

5 Asymmetrical Tonic Neck Reflex
Schilder Test

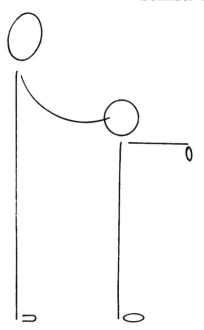

Test position
Standing, feet together, with the arms held straight out at shoulder level and height, but with the hands relaxed at the wrists.

Test procedure
Tester stands behind the subject and gives the instruction: "When I turn your head, I want you to keep your arms straight out in front of you, as they are now. This means your arms remain in the same position, and only your head moves." Tester then slowly rotates the subject's head until the chin is parallel with the shoulder. Pause for 10 seconds. Return the head to the midline. Pause for 10 seconds. Rotate the head to the other side and pause for 10 seconds. Repeat the procedure up to 4 times.

Observations
Any movement of the hand and arm on the side to which the head is turned, i.e. do the arms automatically follow the movement of the head?

Scoring

0	no response
1	slight movement of the arms in the direction the face is pointed
2	movement of the arms in the direction of the head to 45°
3	arm movement to 60°
4	90° rotation of the arms and/or loss of balance as a result of head rotation

6 Rooting Reflex

Emergence: 24-28 weeks in utero
Birth: present
Inhibited: 3-4 months neonate

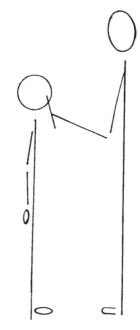

Test position
Standing

Test procedure
Using a small brush, gently stroke from the outer
base of the nose downwards beyond the corner
of the mouth. Repeat two or three times on each side.

Observations
Note any movement or twitching of the mouth in response to the
stimulus, or, withdrawal. Also note any accompanying involuntary
movement of the hands (suggestive of Babkin response).

Scoring

0	no reaction
1	slight twitching of the mouth
2	definite movement of the mouth and/or dislike of the sensation
3	movement and opening of the mouth and/or rubbing of the area stimulated
4	movement of the mouth as if to "smile", opening of the mouth and turning of the head in the direction of the stimulus

7 Suck Reflex

*Repeat procedure as for rooting reflex, but gently stimulate central area
above the upper lip with brush or finger.*

Observations
Involuntary pursing of the lips

Scoring

0	no reaction
1	disproportionate sensation in area stimulated
2	slight movement of the lips
3	pursing of the lips
4	pursing of the lips and tongue movement

8 Spinal Galant Reflex

Emergence: about 20 weeks in utero
Inhibited: 3-9 months of life

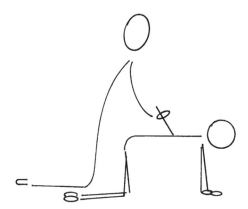

Test position
Four point kneeling or "table" position

Test procedure
Using a light brush, stroke down the back from below the shoulder to the base of the lumbar region at a distance of 1/2 inch from the spine, first on one side, then on the other. Repeat the procedure up to 3 times (repetition beyond this can fail to elicit the reaction even though the reflex is present).

Observations
Movement of the hip outwards in response to stimulation

Scoring
0	no response
1	undulation or movement of the hip outwards to 15°
2	undulation or movement of the hip outwards to 30°
3	undulation or movement of the hip outwards to 45°
4	movement outwards, beyond 45° and may affect the child's balance.

Hypersensitivity—ticklishness—may also be present.

9 Tonic Labyrinthine Reflex (Erect Test)

It should be noted that this test only represents one test in a battery of tests for the tonic labyrinthine reflex. (TLR)

Emerges: Birth
Inhibited: 2-3 months in the prone position,
2-4 months in the supine position, but may still be
present in a weakened form up to the age of 3 years

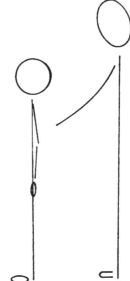

Test position
Standing with feet together, and arms straight
at the sides of the body.

Test procedure
Slowly tilt the subject's head back into extended position and ask the
subject to close the eyes. (Stand behind to support in case there is any
loss of balance). After 10 seconds ask the subject to slowly move the
head forward as if looking at the toes, and maintain that position for a
further 10 seconds. Repeat the sequence 6 times.

Observations
Note any loss of balance or alteration of balance as a result of head
position, or as a result of head movement from above to below the level
of the spine. Also note any compensatory change in muscle tone at the
back of the knees as a result of head movement, or, gripping with the
toes. Ask the subject for any reactions immediately after testing, and
note any comments about dizziness or nausea, both of which suggest
faulty vestibular functioning and/or the residual presence of the tonic
labyrinthine reflex.

Scoring
0	no response
1	slight alteration of balance as a result of head position or movement
2	disturbance of balance during test and/or alteration of muscle tone at the back of the knees
3	near loss of balance, alteration of muscle tone and/or disorientation as a result of the testing procedure
4	loss of balance and/or massive alteration of muscle tone in attempt to maintain balance. This may be accompanied by dizziness or nausea, and in adults, feelings of panic.

10 Symmetrical Tonic Neck Reflex

Emerges: 6-8 months of life
Inhibited: 9-11 months

Figure 1

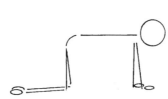

Figure 2

Test position
Four point kneeling "table" position

Test procedure
Subject is instructed to maintain the test position but to slowly move the head to look down "as if looking between your thighs." Hold position for up to 5 seconds and then slowly move the head upwards "as if looking at the ceiling." Repeat up to 6 times.

Observations
Any bending of the arms as a result of head flexion and/or raising of the feet (Fig. 1)

Straightening of the arms and flexion of the knees as a result of head extension (Fig. 2)

Scoring

0	no response
1	tremor in one or both arms or slight hip movement.
2	movement of the elbow on either side and/or definite movement in the hips, or arching of the back
3	bending of the arms on head flexion or movement of the bottom back on head extension
4	bending of the arms to the floor, or movement of the bottom back onto the ankles, so that the subject is sitting in the "cat" position

11 Landau Reflex

Emerges: 2-4 months of life
Inhibited: approximately 3 years of age

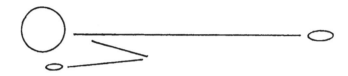

Figure 1

Test position
Prone with arms at right angles to the shoulders (Fig. 1)

Figure 2

Test procedure
Subject is instructed to lift upper trunk, arms and hands off the floor, keeping feet on the floor, and to maintain elevated position for up to 5 seconds. (Fig.2) This may be repeated twice.

Observations
Involuntary lifting of the feet or lower legs as a result of raising the torso.

Scoring
0   no response
1   slight lifting of one or both feet, immediately corrected
2   definite lifting of one or both feet
3   elevation of both feet away from the floor
4   elevation of both feet several inches above the floor and extensor tone throughout the body

12 Amphibian Reflex

Emergence: 4 - 6 months neonatal
Not inhibited.

Test position
First supine, then prone.

Test procedure
1. Ensure subject is completely relaxed.
2. Tester places hands under hip and elevates it to angle of 45°

Observations
As hip is elevated, knee on same side should bend in both supine and prone testing.

Scoring
0.   Knee bends on side of elevated hip.
1.   No visible flexion of knee, but leg remains relaxed.
2.   Leg remains stiff.
3.   Leg is so stiff it begins to lift.
4.   Whole body rolls rigidly

13 Segmental Rolling Reflex

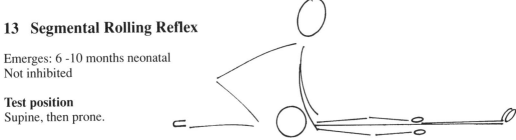

Emerges: 6 -10 months neonatal
Not inhibited

Test position
Supine, then prone.

Test procedure 1
Lift shoulders gently to approximately 45°, at the same time pressing down on the opposite shoulder, and rotate towards opposite side of body.

Observations
As shoulder is lifted, knee on the same side should begin to bend.

Test procedure 2
(Not to be used on cerebral palsy subject.)
Support subject's left heel in left hand.
Apply gentle pressure to bent
left knee with right hand.
Rotate knee slowly across
subject's body until resistance
is met, or the floor is touched.

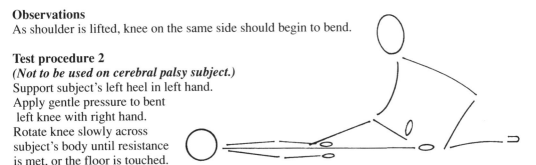

REPEAT PROCEDURE FOR OTHER SIDE.

Observations
Shoulder on same side as rotated knee should begin to lift as knee crosses midline. As knee touches floor, shoulder and arm should follow to complete the rolling over.

Scoring for right and left side separately.

Procedure 1   (Lifting shoulder)
0. Definite bending of knee as shoulder on same side is lifted.
1. Tendency for knee to bend, although it does not do so, as shoulder is lifted
2. Leg remains stationary as shoulder on same side is lifted
3. Entire body and leg lift as shoulder on same side is lifted.
4. No response at all.

Procedure 2   (Pressure on bent knee)
0. Delayed lifting of shoulder, followed by arm and shoulder rolling over to follow knees.
1. Incomplete rotation of shoulder.
2. Shoulder lifts but does not rotate over completely
3. Slight tendency, as the knee crosses the midline, for the shoulder to lift, or the entire body to rotate.
4. No response at all.

14 OCULO-HEADRIGHTING REFLEX

Emergence: 2-3 months neonatal
Not inhibited.

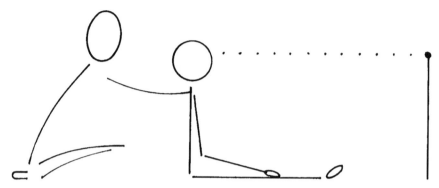

Test Position
Subject seated on floor, legs straight in front, arms resting on thighs.

Test Procedure
1. Subject fixes eyes on an object at eye level.
2. Tester sits behind subject and slowly tilts the subject to the left in
   3 stages, pausing for 2 or 3 seconds at each stage. Pauses are made at
   15°, 30° and 45°. *Note the position of the subject's head at each
   degree of tilt.*
3. Return the subject to the upright sitting position, again in the
   3 stages.
4. Repeat procedure to the right, return to the midline and then
   repeat the procedure backwards and forwards, ensuring that
   the subject keeps the eyes fixed on the object at eye level.

Observations
Head should automatically correct itself to the midline (vertical to the
ground) as the body position is altered in all four directions. Any
flopping of the head or over-compensation in the opposite direction
upon return to the midline position suggests an absent or underdeveloped oculo-headrighting reflex. Also note any extension of the leg
on the side to which the subject is tilted — this may be an indication of
a retained asymmetric tonic neck reflex (ATNR) in the leg.

Scoring
0. Head corrects to the vertical midline position throughout the test.
1. Head slips slightly from the vertical.
2. Head follows direction of the tilt in line with the body.
3. Head leans below the line of the body.
4. Head drops in direction of the tilt.

Lack of headrighting forwards/backwards could indicate underlying
tonic labyrinthine reflex (TLR).

15 LABYRINTHINE HEADRIGHTING REFLEX

Emergence: 2-3 months neonatal
Not inhibited.

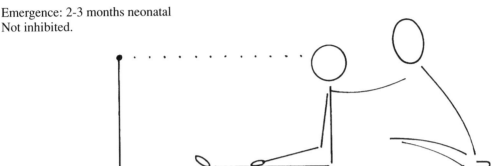

Test Position

Same as for oculo-headrighting reflex, but the subject is asked to fixate his eyes on an object at eye level, and then CLOSE his eyes and to imagine looking at the object during the entire testing procedure.

Test Procedure

1. Subject is instructed to fixate the eyes at eye level object, and then close the eyes and visualize the object throughout the entire testing procedure.
2. Follow the same testing procedure as for oculo-headrighting reflex.

Observations

Note position of the head in all four quadrants, but also note where the subject's closed eyes seem to be directed. (Many children can compensate when their eyes are open, but rapidly lose any sense of where they are in space as soon as the eyes are closed.)

Scoring

0. Head corrects to the vertical midline position throughout the testing
1. Head slips slightly from the vertical
2. Head follows direction of the tilt in line with body
3. Head slips below the line of the body
4. Head drops in the direction of the tilt — no righting apparent.

Also note any compensatory turning of the head — this is NOT the same as automatic righting.

Chapter 6

Remedial Steps Available to the Teacher

Reflex assessment can be used to identify at which level of the child's development remediation should be aimed. Treatment will depend not only upon the severity of the problem but also on the resources—physical conditions, special education experts and remedial programs—available at the school.

If testing shows that a cluster of primitive reflexes are retained, i.e. more than two primitive reflexes are present to 50% or more, then a more detailed reflex assessment should be carried out, and a specific reflex inhibition program devised by a qualified therapist.

A reflex inhibition program is tailored to the reflex profile of the individual child. Progress is monitored at regular intervals and the program adjusted accordingly. Reflex inhibition techniques are based upon the theory of replication: i.e. *it is possible to replicate specific stages of early development through the repetition of movement patterns based upon early development*. The brain is thus given a "second chance" to pass through the developmental stages which were omitted or incomplete in the first year of life, in order to establish neural connections and to set the neural clock to the correct time.

Reflex inhibition movements are based upon very early, primitive movements which the older child would not normally make. *Some children regress both developmentally and emotionally for a short period of time while they are doing such a program*, and for this reason reflex inhibition movements should only be given under careful and qualified supervision.

A specific reflex inhibition program compares to general exercises as a prescription from the pharmacy compares to over-the-counter medication.

Level One

Needs professional help

****

Brainstem level Cerebellum

****

81

Level Two

*Remediation
may be done
in school or
at home*

****

*(Brainstem)
Midbrain
Cerebellum*

****

If it has been determined that the child has underdeveloped postural reflexes (there will be minimal evidence of primitive reflexes) the child will respond well to a motor training program designed to stimulate the postural reflexes and to improve balance and coordination.

Specialists such as occupational therapists or "sensory integration" therapists may work with an individual child in this way, or, general exercises can be incorporated into special gym classes or even be given to a child to practice daily at home under parental supervision.

> *Sensory integration is based on a system of therapy devised by A. Jean Ayres using sensory input techniques combined with movement to enhance the clarity of incoming information via each of the senses. It strives for efficient transmission of information via the central nervous system (CNS), and the development of more mature patterns of response.*
>
> *There are many excellent motor training programs available, which can be used within the school system e.g. Kephart, Cratty, Dennison, Lefroy and many others.*

Within the school environment, both the physical education teacher and the music teacher may be able to provide invaluable input for the "borderline" child. The physical education classes allow opportunities to improve motor skills and balance. Music classes sharpen auditory discrimination and increase vocal and rhythmic skills. The use of sound opens an alternative route to memory and sequencing skills for those children who do not respond to the methods taught in the regular classroom. A child does not have to be a potential musical prodigy to benefit from both simple and advanced listening and vocalizing exercises.

See Table III for suggested activities

Once the rules and mechanics of normal development are understood, a suitable program of motor and sensory stimulation can be put together. As a general guide normal development follows a set sequence — vestibular, tactile, auditory, visual, proprioceptive. One system is built upon and integrated with the others. Each relies upon instantaneous feedback. Deficit or hypersensitivity in one channel will affect the operation of the others. Development also follows a cephalo-caudal (head to toe) and proximo-distal (from the center outwards) course. Any attempt at physical remediation should take this into account.

SENSORY DIFFICULTIES: AUDITORY

The child who has problems in auditory processing will often respond to sound therapy.

An increasing number of methods are currently available, all of which operate upon a common principle that language skills such as speech, reading, writing, spelling and musical expression can only develop if the child has learned to "listen". Advanced listening involves both the exclusion of irrelevant sounds and the ability to focus upon a specific sound. In this respect, effective listening resembles good vision. The following list is only intended as a guide to help decide which method may be relevant for a particular child:

Cortex
Corpus callosum
Midbrain
Brainstem

a) Dyslexia, reading, spelling and articulation difficulties:
   Auditory Discrimination Training—Dr. Kjeld Johansen
b) Autism, aphasia, language and general learning difficulties:
   Auditory Integrative Training—Dr. Guy Berard
c) Listening, language and general learning difficulties, the need to fine-tune musical skills and unexplained anxiety:
   The Tomatis Method— individual centers
   Samonas center—Dr. I. Steinbach

(Johansen and Steinbach can be used within school or home environment)

The music teacher is the ally in overcoming auditory problems. The child who has poor listening skills may have a monotone voice, lack of cadence in speech and have a poor sense of pitch and rhythm. (This is a vestibular problem.)

Mainly cortical but also midbrain and brainstem

Provide simple exercises which involve listening. Play two notes and then teach the child to "hear" which one is higher, and practice to judge the difference or interval between them. Do two notes played together clash or harmonize? What is the difference in interval between sounds which blend and sounds which clash? Even if the child cannot sing in tune, encourage the child to sing each note and record on a tape recorder and then modify his singing after listening to the sound of his own voice. Encourage the singing of simple rhymes and sequences to tunes e.g. days of the week, months of the year, tables, alphabet, etc.

An entire system of general teaching is now available based upon the concept of the "selfvoice". The system ARROW, which is an acronym for Aural-Reading-Respond-Oral-Written requires the child to read a section of text into a special tape recorder. He has to listen to the sound of his own voice, then to rewind and use his own voice to dictate. He also writes down the relevant information. Vast improvements in reading and spelling age are noticeable in only a few weeks of use.

For many children a tune can act as a code to a memory filing system, and thus provide an alternative method of accessing information. These are only a few preliminary ideas upon which other more sophisticated exercises could be based.

SENSORY PROBLEMS: VISUAL

If oculomotor or visual-perceptual problems are detected, but are unrelated to aberrant reflexes, the advice of an optometrist specializing in Behavioral or Developmental Optometry should be sought, who may be able to suggest exercises which can be used by the entire classroom.

Cortical

See also
Table III

83

SENSORY PROBLEMS: KINESTHETIC

See also
Table III

The Physical Education teacher should be informed if deficit in this area has been found. Table III links specific types of movement to individual reflexes. These could be built into a movement routine to be used with a class on a regular basis over several months, or could be given to one child to practice daily at home. Unlike most physical education classes, where the aim is to build musculature and improve fitness, these exercises should be performed slowly and deliberately to allow time for feedback between the afferent and efferent systems.

GENERAL AWARENESS

While the class teacher is usually too busy with the daily curriculum, there are methods to make it easier to cope with the variety of skill levels to which to adjust teaching. Table III has suggestions which may be used by all teachers, but the following strategies outlined by Jane Field (1992) may also help to accommodate the neuro-developmentally delayed child in the classroom.

1. Moro Reflex

A most important accommodation that a teacher can make for a child with an aberrant Moro reflex is to create a classroom with as non-threatening an environment as possible. This can be done by keeping the general noise levels to a minimum: both her own and that of the children. General movement levels should also be reduced as much as possible, so that the eyes are more able to attend selectively to what is of immediate concern to them. Careful planning can seat certain children in positions where much of the general bustle of the classroom is outside their field of vision.

All children hate to be singled out —to be different— unless that difference increases status with their peers. The child with a Moro reflex feels at variance with others and has difficulty fitting into a group. As a result his self-esteem is usually low, or at best, fragile. A teacher who is aware of such a trait and understands the underlying reason, can do much to build confidence without making the child feel conspicuous.

2. Tonic Labyrinthine Reflex

The child with a retained tonic labyrinthine reflex (TLR) will have spatial and organizational difficulties and will respond best to well ordered, precise information. He may have difficulty forming concepts and will probably need to use concrete objects to understand and solve problems which other children can tackle through abstract reasoning. Oculomotor and directional problems may make arithmetic particularly difficult as alignment of figures is crucial both for finding the correct answer and for understanding the principle of hundreds, tens and units.

This is where simple strategies such as the use of squared paper and ruled columns will help prevent confusion. A marker or guiding finger may help with reading to reduce mistakes caused by poor tracking skills. The child who is visually "stimulus bound" may find that a card with a "window cut-out" will help to minimize distraction from the rest of the page.

3. Asymmetrical Tonic Neck Reflex

The child who still has an ATNR needs extra space to write in order to accommodate the effect of the reflex. This is the child who may rotate the page by as much a 90° to allow for the fact that every time he turns his head to write, his arm wants to stretch. He often pushes the paper to the far side of the working surface. Seating a right and a left handed child together at a table will cause enormous problems for this child. If, in addition, the child also has retained a Moro reflex, then the distractions of "group teaching" may make concentration impossible for him. Simple changes such as arranging the classroom for at least some individual desks or placing tables in rows facing the teacher, will help to minimize distraction and allow each child maximum personal space. Difficulty with the physical act of writing will prevent the child from being able to express ideas in written form while it is easy for him to do so orally. Ideas can be reinforced by allowing a period of discussion which can then be condensed into key words or phrases as an outline for an essay or a short piece of creative writing. Similarly, the child can be taught to underline salient points in a paragraph meant to test his comprehension, so that he has instant access or referral to the main points for discussion.

Use of typewriters or computers can aid spelling, grammar and content, as the child is freed from the physical constraints of the ATNR to use his intelligence more effectively. "Spellchecks" on the computer will help to reinforce correct spelling and thereby develop visual memory for difficult words. Where improvement in handwriting is essential, some of a child's homework may be done on a computer, and then the correct version copied by hand into the exercise book. Simple aids such as a "marker" for reading, will help to prevent frequent loss of place where eye tracking is erratic.

4 . Symmetrical Tonic Neck Reflex

This is the child whose posture will be affected by any movement of his head forwards or backwards. This will be particularly devastating when the child sits at a desk, as inclining the head forward to focus on work will cause the arms to bend and the head to fall nearer and nearer to the working surface. The effect of this can be minimized by altering the angle of the work surface so that the head can be maintained in a more erect posture. The old fashioned sloping desks were ideal for this, but a triangular structure which can be placed on top of the table will have the same effect.

The effects of the symmetrical tonic neck reflex (STNR) will usually diminish quickly if a motor training program is given. Such a program would include slow rocking on hands and knees in response to head movement, and short periods of crawling and of creeping .

SUMMARY

The presence of a primitive or lack of postural reflex at key stages in development may be seen as evidence of continuing subcortical control over neuromuscular functions. Voluntary control of movement directly reflects the degree of cortical control in the individual—the cortex represents purposive behavior whereas subcortical behavior is limited and stereotyped. Subcortical systems may remain dominant for a number of reasons: lack of use at an early stage in development; lack of inhibition; metabolic or pathological conditions, or possibly directly through injury. Any of the above can interfere with cortical functioning at a later stage. Detection and analysis of primitive and postural reflexes can therefore be used as a valuable tool in assessing the level of remediation required by a child, as it indicates the developmental stage a child has reached. Being able to pinpoint this exact stage helps to determine the teaching method from which a child is likely to benefit the most.

The reflexes, however, provide only the substrata for later learning, and by the time that a child has reached the age of 8 years, other systems will also have become involved. The reflexes are only one sign of misdirection in development, which may then be accompanied by dysfunctions in the processing of auditory information, visual information, vestibular functioning, etc.

It is therefore important to examine which area presents the greatest stumbling block for the individual child and to devise a personalized program. For, although the symptoms of dysfunction may be similar for many children, the developmental route the child has had to take to compensate for his problems, is as individual as he is. This is why a battery of tests can be invaluable in assessing the needs of the individual child.

The key areas of investigation should include tests for:
>   Gross muscle coordination and balance
>   Cerebellar functioning
>   Both primitive and postural reflexes
>   Laterality
>   Oculomotor and visual-perceptual functioning
>   Auditory discrimination skills and auditory laterality
>   Performance on specific age related tasks

The teacher should also be aware of the possibility of other factors which may also be part of the overall problem: poor nutrition and allergies, detrimental social environment, genetic or metabolic influences, and psychological problems.

A developmental approach enables the teacher/therapist/psychologist to "take the lid off learning difficulties" and look again at the question posed by Tansley over 20 years ago: *"For far too long teachers have concentrated upon the psychological problems of the child, or the socio-economic environment, instead of asking the question, does the child have the equipment which he needs to succeed at the educational level asked of him and methods imposed on him?"*

It was this question which, twenty years ago, first led Peter Blythe into the search for a physical basis to learning difficulties. These methods were then taken to Sweden and developed by Catharina Johannsen Alvegård in the late 1970s, to the United States in the 1980s, and Germany in the 1990s and are now incorporated into many teachers' "thinking" throughout the world. For if the basic equipment essential for learning is made strong, then teaching methods can become effective and the child can start to grow. In our modern world, there is little room for academic failure, and if it seems to exist we must continue to ask the question "WHY?"

Table I

DEVELOPMENT AND TRANSFORMATION OF THE REFLEX SYSTEM

REFLEX	EMERGES	INHIBITION	TRANSFORMATION
1. Uterine withdrawal re-flexes	5-7 weeks in utero	9-32 weeks in utero	Moro reflex
2. Moro reflex	9-12 weeks in utero	2-4 months neonate	Adult 'startle' response (Strauss reflex)
3. Palmar reflex	11 weeks in utero	2-3 months neonate	Voluntary release progres-sing to a 'pincer' grip
4. Plantar reflex	11 weeks in utero	7-9 months neonate	Adult Plantar
5. Asymmetrical Tonic Neck reflex	c. 18 weeks in utero	3-9 months neonate	Transformed tonic neck reflex
6. Spinal Galant reflex	20 weeks in utero	3-9 months neonate	Amphibian reflex
7. Rooting reflex and 8. Suck reflex	24-28 weeks in utero	3-4 months neonate	Adult suck reflex and sub-sequent development of mature sucking and swall-owing movements essen-tial for speech and clear-articulation
9. Tonic labyrinthine re-flex forwards	12 weeks in utero	3-4 months neonate	Head-righting reflex Landau reflex
10. TLR-backwards	Emerges at birth	2-4 months neonate	Head-righting reflexes
11. Babinski reflex	1 week neonate	12-24 months	Adult Plantar
12. Stepping reflex	1 week neonate	6 months	Inhibited by 6 months at the latest
13. Abdominal reflex	4 weeks neonate	remains	Is indicative of increasing maturity in the upper pyra-midal tract and thus is associated with balance and muscle tone
14. Landau reflex	4-6 weeks neonate	3 years	Control of balance between flexor and extensor muscles
15. Head-righting reflexes	2-4 months	remains	The basis of balance, oculomotor functioning orientation and spatial awareness

Table II

HISTORICAL INDICATORS OF NEURO-DEVELOPMENTAL DELAYS

PREGNANCY
- Hyperemesis (severe sickness)
- Severe viral infection during the first 12 weeks or between 26 and 30 weeks
- Excessive alcohol consumption and/or drug abuse
- Radiation
- Accident or infection
- Threatened miscarriage
- Hypertension
- Placental insufficiency (small for dates)
- Smoking
- Toxoplasmosis
- Severe stress
- Uncontrolled diabetes

BIRTH
- Prolonged labor or precipitive labor
- Placenta previa
- High forceps or ventouse extraction
- Breech
- Cesarian
- Cord around the neck
- Fetal distress
- Premature (more than 2 weeks early) or post mature (more than 2 weeks late)

NEWBORN DISORDERS
- Low birth weight (under 5 lbs.)
- Incubation
- Distorted skull
- Prolonged jaundice
- Requiring rescusitation
- Blue baby
- Heavy bruising
- Problems with feeding the first 6 months

INFANCY
- Illnesses involving a high fever, delirium or convulsions in the first 18 months
- Adverse reaction to any of the innoculations
- Late at learning to walk (later than 18 months)
- Late at learning to talk (later than 18 months)
- Difficulty learning to dress, eg. buttons, tie shoelaces, etc.
- Thumb sucking up until the age of 5 years or more
- Bed-wetting above the age of 5 years
- History of repeated ear, nose or throat infections
- Severe allergic reactions

CHILDHOOD & SCHOOL HISTORY
- Travel sickness—headache or nausea, especially while reading in car, boat or plane.
- Difficulty learning to ride a two wheel bicycle
- Difficulty learning to read
- Difficulty learning to write, or in making the transition from printing to cursive script
- Difficulty in learning to tell the time (clock face v. digital clock)
- Poor hand-eye coordination
- Mixed handedness if still present above the age of 8 years
- Inability to sit still or to remain silent up to the age of 11 or 12 years
- Difficulty in physical education classes: e.g. forward roll, handstands, cartwheels, climbing a rope, and other signs of general clumsiness and lack of coordination.
- Difficulty learning to swim
- Speech and articulation problems

Rarely will a single factor by itself indicate Neuro-Developmental Delay. As with primitive reflexes, it is only where a <u>cluster</u> of factors exist that NDD may be present. Indicators of NDD are not limited to the above list.

TABLE III

REMEDIATION FOR RETAINED REFLEXES

Reflex	School Problem	Remediation Approach

Moro Reflex
Test:
1. Head drop in supine
2. Drop back test
	Over-reactive
	Hypersensitive
	Stimulus bound
	Difficulty with ball games
		Sensory: Vestibular training,
		   tactile stimulation,
		   sound therapy

Palmar Reflex Test: 1. Stimulation of the palm of the hand	Poor manual dexterity Immature pencil grip Speech and hand move- ments may be connected	Exercises: A) Clasping and unclasping of the hand around an object; B) Independent thumb movement progressing to thumb opposition and finger movements; C) Finger exercises with hands separately and then making different movements with hands together.
Asymmetrical Tonic Neck Reflex Test: 1. Supine, head rotation 2. Schilder test	Handwriting; expression of ideas in written form; eye tracking problems; Difficulty crossing the midline; ambilaterality or cross laterality	1) Slow exercises which begin with homolateral movements of the body in response to head rotation in same direction while lying supine; Progress to extension of one side of body in opposite direction to head rotation; Independent cross pattern movement of arms and legs with head at midline. These should be performed in slow motion while lying on the back. 2) Develop eye tracking movements by asking the child to slowly move the thumb of the dominant hand from side-to-side at a distance of 8-10" from the face, keeping the head still while focusing on the thumb. First, ask the child to do this with eyes closed, imagining he is focusing on his thumb, six times, then repeat with the eyes open. 3) Slowly move thumb back and forth from near-point to arm's length while focusing on thumb. Extend the distance of focus to a spot on the wall and then back to the thumb again at arm's length and near-poin
Rooting and Suck Test: Stimulation of the two sides of the mouth.	Poor articulation, prolonged thumb sucking, messy eating, dribbling; oversensitive to touch on the face; possible need for orthodontic treatment later; Swallowing movements too near the front of the mouth may develop a high palate and narrow jaw.	Reflex Inhibition Program
Spinal Galant Test: Stimulation of the lumbar region.	Inability to sit still or remain silent; poor concentration; continued bed wetting above the age of 5 years.	Reflex Inhibition Program if present with other primitive reflexes. If it is the only retained primitive reflex, exercises done lying on the back will inhibit the pelvic tilting.
Tonic Labyrinthine Test: Movement of the head through the vertical plane, forward and backward beyond the midline.	Poor balance; rigid or floppy muscle (seen in P.E. when running); oculo-motor dysfunctions: a) tracking, b) convergence, c) reestablishment of binocular vision. Visual-perceptual difficulties. Possible auditory problems. Organizational problems, poor sense of time and rhythm.	1) Vestibular stimulation, ie. rotation, rolling and rocking initially done with the eyes closed; 2) Stretching and flexion exercises performed on the floor in supine and prone with eyes closed TLR present above a test score of 2 in conjunction with any other reflex inhibition exercises.

TABLE III *(continued)*

REMEDIATION FOR RETAINED REFLEXES

Reflex	School Problem	Remediation Approach

Symmetrical Tonic
Test:
  Head extension and
  flexion in table position.
	Posture: lies on desk when writing. Poor eye-hand co-ordination; problems with refocusing from far to near distance. Clumsy.	Creeping on hands and knees; provide a sloping or tilted desk surface.

Posturals — Absent or under-developed:		
Head-Righting Test:	Oculo-motor dysfunctions, visual-perceptual difficulties. Poor spatial awareness. Motion sickness.	Vestibular training, eg. slow rotation (eyes closed), rolling and tilting, progressing to eyes open as balance and head-righting improves. Scooter board, wobble board, first lying, then sitting, then standing; and using trampoline.
Landau Reflex Test:	Imbalance between extensor and flexor	Prone — lifting torso off the ground while keeping feet on the ground.
Amphibian and Segmental Rolling Test:	Lack of segmental or differentiated movement through the body.	Rolling from prone to supine and vice-versa, initiating movement from one portion of the body, i.e. bend one leg and slowly bring across the body to stimulate rolling of upper portion of body.
Equilibrium Reactions		These will only develop fully if the Moro and Tonic Labyrinthine reflexes are inhibited; absence of equilibrium reactions may be symptomatic of other retained primitive reflexes.

Appendix 1

Useful Addresses

The Institute for Neuro-Physiological Psychology is responsible for the research, clinical practice and management of neuro-developmental therapy (NDT). There are also therapists practicing throughout the UK who operate as Associates of the Institute.

The Institute for Neuro-Physiological Psychology (INPP)   www.inpp.org.uk
Peter Blythe
Warwick House
4 Stanley Place
Chester CH1 2LU, UK
Tel & Fax: 01244 311414

In addition to the main training course for therapists, INPP also runs one day courses for teachers and other professionals in the use of the screening questionnaire, and a small test battery and series of developmental games that can be used with small or large groups of children in a class setting.

The International School for Research and Training in Neuro-Developmental Delay is responsible for the training of all professionals wishing to practice reflex inhibition therapy as devised by The Institute for Neuro-Physiological Psychology.
For further information on training and seminars, contact:

The International School for Training and Research in Neuro-Developmental Delay
4 Stanley Place
Chester CH1 2LU, UK
Tel & Fax: 01244 311414

Associated organizations practicing INPP techniques include:

Sweden
1.   The Swedish Institute for Neuro-Physiological Psychology
        Catharina Johanneson Alvegård
        Rydholmsgat. 42
        S41873, Gothenberg
        Sweden
Catharina Johanneson Alvegård is also responsible for all training within Sweden.

2.   Hakaan Carlsson Sensomotoriskt Centrum
        Blaklintskolan
        Martensgatan 12
        595 32 Mjolby, Sweden
        Fax 0142 852 86
3.   Vestibularis
        Mats and Irene Niklasson
        Parkgatan 11
        S38331 Monsterås, Sweden

Netherlands
> The Dutch Institute for Neuro-
> Physiological Psychology
> Jur Ten Hoopen
> Amsteldyk 138, Netherlands

USA
> Dr. Larry Beuret, MD
> 4811 Emerson Suite 209
> Palatine, Illinois 60067, USA

Germany
> Pedagogische Praxis
> Thake Hansen Lauff
> An der Heide 1
> 24235 Wendtorfer Schleuse, Germany

Australia
> Dr. Mary Lou Shiel
> 80 Alexandra Street
> Hunters Hill 2110
> Sydney, Australia

> ANSUA - Children's Learning
> & Development Center
> Maureen Hawke
> 333 Given Terrace
> Rosalie
> Queensland, Australia

SOUND THERAPY CENTERS

Dyslexia Research Laboratory
Dr. Kjeld Johansen
Ro/ Skolovej 14 DK 3760
Gudhjem, Bornholm, Denmark

The Tomatis Center UK Ltd
3 Wallands Crescent
Lewes
East Sussex BN7 2QT, UK

The Listening Center (Tomatis Method)
Paul Madaule
599 Markham Street
Toronto, Canada M6G 2L7

Auditory Integrative Training (Dr. Guy Berard)
Information available from:
The Georgiana Foundation
PO Box 2607, Westport
CT 06880, USA

Samonas (Dr. I. Steinbach)
Klangstudio LAMBDOMA
Markengrafenufer 9
59071 Hamm, Germany

OPTOMETRY

Further information and addresses available
from:
> Optometric Extension Program
> Foundation, Inc.
> Vision West Inc.
> 1921 E Carnegie Avenue, Suite 3L
> Santa Ana, CA 92705, USA

> College of Optometrists In Vision
> Development
> P. O. Box 285
> Chula Vista, CA 91912-0285

READING DIFFICULTIES

> The Arrow Trust
> Dr. Colin Lane
> The Priory Annexe
> St. Mary Street
> Bridgewater, Somerset TA6 3EK, UK
> Fax: 01278 446261

AUTISM

> Autism Research Institute
> Bernard Rimland, Ph.D.
> 4182 Adams Avenue
> San Diego, CA 921169, USA

Appendix 2

References

American Psychiatric Association, (1994) *Diagnostic and Statistical Manual of Mental Disorders.* (DSM IV) Washington, DC.

American Psychiatric Association, (1980) *DSM III*, Washington, DC.

Arnheim, R.,(1969) *Visual thinking.* University of California Press, Berkely, CA.

Ayres, A.J., (1979/82) *Sensory integration and the child.* Western Psychological Services, Los Angeles, CA.

Bainbridge, Cohen, B., (1993) *Sensing, feeling and action.* Contact Editions, P.O. Box 603, Northampton, MA 01061

Bennett, R., (1988) *The hidden Moro.* Private publication.

Bakker, D.J., (1990) *Neurophysiological treatment of dyslexia.* Oxford University Press Inc.

Beuret, Lawrence, (1989) personal communication.

Blythe, P., (1971) *Hypnotism, its power and practice.* Arthur Barker, London.

Blythe, P. (1976) *Self Hypnotism.* Arthur Barker, London and Taplinger, NY.

Blythe, P. (1990) *A physical basis for panic disorder.* Lecture at the 4th International Conference of Neurological Dysfunction in Children and Adults. Guernsey, C.I., UK, September, 1990.

Blythe, P. and McGlown, D.J., (1979) *An organic basis for neuroses and educational difficulties.* Insight Publications, 4 Stanley Place, Chester, England.

Blythe, P., (1992) Personal communication.

Bobath, K. and Bobath B., (1955) *Tonic reflexes and righting reflexes in the diagnosis and assessment of Cerebral Palsy.* Cerebral Palsy Bulletin, May 16, l955.

Bobath, B., (1975) *Abnormal postural reflex activity caused by brain lesions.* William Heineman, London

Brain, W. B., (1987) *Brain's clinical neurology.* Revised by Bannister, R., Oxford Medical Publications, Oxford.

Brunnstrom, S., (1962) *Training the adult hemiplegic patient: orientation of techniques to patients' motor behaviour.* In: Approaches to treatment of patients with neuromotor dysfunction. 3rd International Congress, World Federation of Occupational Therapists.

Capute, A. (1986) *Early neuro-motor reflexes in infancy.* Pediatric Annals, March 15, l986.

Capute, A., Shapiro B.K. Palmer, F.B., Accardo, P.J. Wachtel, R.C., (1981) *Primitive reflexes, a factor in non-verbal language in early infancy.* Language Behaviour in Infancy and Early Childhood. (Ed. Stark.) Elsevier North Holland, Rue, Netherlands.

95

Cottrell, S., (1987) *Aetiology, diagnosis and treatment of asthma through primitive reflex inhibition*. Presented at the 2nd International Conference of Neurological dysfunction. Stockholm, 1988.

Cratty, B.J., (1973) *Movement, behavior and motor learning*. Henry Kimpton Publishers, London.

Delacato, C.H., (1959) *The treatment and prevention of reading problems*. Charles C. Thomas, Springfield, Illinois.

Delacato, C. H., (1974) *The ultimate stranger, the autistic child*. Academic Therapy Publications, Novato, CA.

DeMyer, W. (1980), *Techniques of the neurological examination*. McGraw-Hill, New York.

Dennison, P.E., (1981) *Switching on*. Edu-Kinesthetics, Glendale, CA.

Dickson, V. Personal communication.

Draper, I.T., (1993) *Lecture notes on neurology*. Blackwell Scientific Publications, Oxford.

Duighan, (1994) personal communication.

Eustis, R.S., (1947) *The primary origin of the specific language disability*. Journal of Pediatrics XXXI (1947)

Fay, T., (1942) quoted in Doman G., Le Winn, E.B., Wilkinson, R., (1977) Temple Fay revisited: *"The other side of the fit." A bill of particulars on seizures and on discontinuing anticonvulsant drugs*. The In-Report. Vol V, no. 6, 1977.

Field, J., (1992) *Accommodating the neuro-developmentally delayed child within the classroom*. Field Publications, Gatepiece Cottage, Highfields, Wichenford, Worcs, WR6 6YG, UK.

Field J. and Blythe, P., (1988) *Towards developmental re-education*. Field Publication, Gatepiece Cottage, Highfield, Wickenford, Worcester, UK.

Fiorentino, M.R.,(1981) *Reflex testing methods for evaluating C.N.S. development*. Bannerstonem House, 301327 East Lawrence Ave., Springfield, Ill.

Gaddes, W.H., (1980) *Learning disabilities and brain function: a neurophysical approach*. Springer Verlag, New York .

Galaburda, A.M., LeMay, M., Kemper, T.L. Geschwind, N., (1978) *Right/left asymmetries in the brain*. Harvard University Press, Massachusetts.

Galley, P.M. & Forster, A.L., (1982) *Human movement*. Churchill Livingston, Edingburgh.

Gesell A., (1947) Part 1, *The first five years of life*. A guide to the study of pre-school children. Wathuen, 36 Essex Street, Strand. London.

Gesell, A. and Ames, L., (1947) *The development of handedness*, Journal of Genetic Psychology, 70. 1947 pp . 155-75.

Gilfoyle, E., Grady A. & Moore, J. (1972) *Children adapt*. Ch. Slack Inc. 6900 Grove Rd. Thorofare, N.J.

Goddard, S., (1989) *The Fear paralysis response and its interaction with the primitive reflexes*. INPP Monograph Series., No.1, 1989, Chester, England.

Goddard. S., (1989) *The fear paralysis reflex and its interactions with the primitive reflexes*. Private publication.

Gold, S. J., (1986) *When children invite child abuse*. Fern Ridge Press, Eugene, Oregon.

Hocking, B., (1990) *Little boy lost.* Bloomsbury Publishing Ltd, London.

Holt, K.S., (1991) *Child Development.* Butterworth-Heineman, London.

Johansen, K.V., (1993) Lyd, *Horelseog sprogudvikling.* Dyslexia Research Lab. Ro Skolovej 14 DK 3760, Gudhjem, Bornholm, Denmark.

Johansen, K.V., (1992) *Sensory deprivation—a possible cause of dyslexia.* Nordisk Tidsskrift for Spesialpedagogikk, Scandinavian University Press, Abonementssekjonen, Postboks 2959, Toyen, N-0608 Oslo, Norge.

Kaada, B., (1986) *Sudden Infant Death Syndrome.* Oslo University Press.

Kephart, N.C., (1960) *The slow learner in the classroom.* Merrill, Columbus, Ohio.

Kermoian, Rosanne, (1988) *Locomotor experience: A facilitator of spatial cognitive development.* Child Development, Aug. 1988, Vol. 59.

Laborit, H., (1952) As quoted in Odent. M. *Birth reborn.*

Lefroy, R., (1990) *Improving literacy through motor development.* Dunsborough Enterprises. Pty Ltd Publications, P.O. Box 134, Palmyra, W. Australia 6157.

Levinson, H.L., (1984) *Smart but feeling dumb.* Warner Books Inc., New York.

Machover, I. (1990) Personal communication.

MacLean, P., (1978) *A mind of three minds: educating the triune brain.* The National Society for the Study of Education, Chicago.

Madaule, P., (1993) *When listening comes alive.* Moulin Publishing, Box # 560, Ontario L0P 1K0.

Martin, M., Grover B., (1990) *Ears and hearing.* Macdonald & Co. Ltd., Orbit House, London

Merck Manual, (1987) *The manual of diagnosis and therapy* (15th edition) Merck, Sharp & Dohme Research Laboratories.

Odent, M., (1991) Paper presented at The European Conference of Neuro-developmental Delay.

Odent, M., (1986) *Primal Health,* Century, Hutchinson, London.

Odent, M., (1984) *Birth reborn.* Souvenir Press, London.

O'Reilly, B. (1990) *The role of phenolic and related compounds as a possible causative factor in autism—a hypothesis.* Private publication.

Pavlidis, G., Miles, T., (1987) *Dyslexia research and its applications to education.* Wiley Publications.

Pyfer, J., Johnson R. (1981) *Factors affecting motor delays.* Extract from Adapted Physical Activity. Eason, Smith & Caron, Human Kinetics Publishers, Box 5076, Champaign, Ill. 61820.

Restak, R., (1991) *The brain has a mind of its own.* Harmony Books, New York.

Reuven, Kohen-Raz, (1986) *Learning disabilities and postural control.* Freund Publishing House Ltd. Suite 500, Chesham House, 150 Regent Street, London . W1R 5PA.

Shepherd, R., (1990) *Physiotherapy in Pediatrics.* Butterworth-Heineman, Oxford.

Smith, J., (1993) Illustrations. Flexton Bank, Tilston, Malpas, England.

Southall, D.P., Samuels, M.P. & Talbert, D.G., (1990) *Recurrent cyanotic episodes with severe arterial hypoxaemia and intrapulmonary shunting: a mechanism for sudden death.* Archives of Disease in Childhood. 65:953-961, 1990.

Steinbach, I., (1994) *How does sound therapy work?* Paper presented at *The 6th European Conference of Neuro-Developmental Delay in Children with Specific Learning Difficulties.* Klangstudio Lambdoma, Markgrafenufer 9, 59071 Hamm, Germany.

Storr, A., (1993) *Music and the mind.* Harper Collins, 77-85 Fulham Palace Road, London W6 8JB

Tansley, A.E., (1967) *Reading and remedial reading.* Routledge and Kegan Paul Ltd. London.

Telleus, C., (1980) *En komarativ studie av neurologisk skillnader hos barn medoch utan läs-och skrivovarigheter.* Götheborg Universitet, Psychologisker Instituktionen.

Thelan, F., (1979), *Rhythmical stereotypes in normal human infants.* Animal Behavior, 1979, No. 27, pp.699-715.

Tomatis, A.A., (1991) *The conscious ear.* Station Hill Press Inc. Barrytown, New York 12507
Tomatis. A.A. (1991) *About the Tomatis method.* The Listening Centre. 600 Markham Street, Toronto, Ontario, M6G 2LG.

Tomatis, A.A., (1980) *Audio-psycho-phonology: a new challenge.* Lecture given at Potchefstrom University, Republic of South Africa, April, 1980.

Trevor-Roper, P., (1987) *The world through blunted vision.* Penguin, London.

Veras, R., (1975) *Children of dreams, children of hope.* Henry Regnery, Chicago.

Williamson, (1992) *The Brain: science opens new windows on the mind.* Newsweek, April 1992.

Wisbey, A. , (1977) *Sounding out dyslexia.* World Medicine, October 1977.

Appendix 3

Papers

ELECTIVE MUTISM: THE UNCHOSEN SILENCE !

The term "selective mutism" formerly described as "elective mutism" infers a voluntary refusal to speak in certain situations. DSM IV (1995)—with a cross reference from ELECTIVE MUTISM—describes its characteristics as follows:

"The essential feature of selective mutism is the persistent failure to speak in specific social situations, (e.g. school, with playmates) where speaking is expected, despite speaking in other situations. (This diagnosis should not be given if it lasts for less than a month, the child has no knowledge of the subject being discussed, or suffers from other forms of language or developmental disorders, or schizophrenia.) Instead of communicating by standard verbalization, children with this disorder may communicate by gestures, nodding or shaking the head, or pulling or pushing, or in some cases by monosyllabic, short or monotone utterances, or in an altered voice."

"Associated features include: Excessive shyness, fear of social embarrassment, social isolation and withdrawal, clinging, compulsive traits, temper tantrums or other controlling or oppositional behavior, particularly in the home."

Selective/elective mutism is a separate condition from autism, but in certain circumstances it might be viewed as a minor form of autism or a manifestation of a particular autistic type of behavior. One autistic 17 year old who had been unable to talk since the age of 6, was later able to write down her experiences of being locked in the silent world. (Hocking. 1990)

(The following original text was written without punctuation of any kind. Minimal punctuation has been inserted by the writer to facilitate easier reading.)

"Caroline wanted to talk so much. but it seemed to be an impossible task. "Do you think she will ever talk?" was the question that everyone always asked her mother and her teacher, to which they replied. "There is no reason why she shouldn't. All the apparatus is there. She used to talk when she was a little girl."

Some people found this hard to believe. They thought her parents must be deluding themselves and that she had always been silent. But she had spoken. She could remembers quite clearly the times she had said things to her Mommy. "Look at the moon" she said one day, caught by the sudden beauty of it in the daytime sky. She must have been about six years old at the time, lost in her

99

misery, but still responsive to beauty coming unawares from the heavens. She could remember other times when she had tried to say things, but had been caught in the black web of her unhappiness and unable to utter a sound. It is very difficult to explain the way in which her fear gripped her vocal chords. It felt as though unseen hands were pressing on her throat struggling to extinguish life itself. Such a little place for the air to come and go, and so little room for the mysterious life force to exist. That area of her body seemed so especially vulnerable, so very exposed, that it must be protected at all costs, even the cost of silence. It seemed to save valuable air for the process of life itself. There was none to spare for eventual speech, so speech had to go. No one realized that this was one of the fears behind the silence: this sense of tight breathlessness that seemed to suffocate and threaten what little life there was with extinction. This was a real feeling when she was a tiny girl, but it was not until she was nearly grown up that she had the detachment to describe it. It was the same with so many feelings now that she was older. She could give a description to the things that had hurled great doubts and fears at her small mind. She had the words to describe what it had all been like that's why she felt it was so important to write a book to explain. As her teacher had said, she was in a position to help others. Real experience, ably described, was worth a ton of suppositions by wellmeaning experts. What hurt so much, was the widely held belief that students of psychiatry seemed to hold, if you were silent you could not understand. If you didn't use language you couldn't express any thoughts. But how did they know that a lot of speechless people hadn't got heads full of beautiful expressive language that they couldn't use, because no one had found the key to their confidence."

It would be very easy to analyze this girl's feelings in terms of psychological etiology, but it is the purpose of this paper to argue that elective mutism has an underlying physical basis and to examine the underlying mechanisms which in certain situations might inhibit the organs of speech production.

Two of the most powerful images that this girl's description evokes are those of fear and of breathlessness. Many phrases in the English language imply a connection between fear and the inability to talk: "petrified", "speechless with fear", "frozen to the spot", "tongue tied" and "struck dumb" —each one a recognition of a normal, momentary response to extreme fear. The question that poses itself here is: Why should certain individuals experience such extreme fear in the course of their day-to-day living, even to the extent that they cannot operate or interact effectively with the outside world?

An explanation may be found within the concept of neuro-developmental delay (NDD). Neuro-developmental delay encompasses a variety of symptoms, of which elective mutism may be one. These symptoms emanate from an arrested or omitted stage of development during either the fetal or the infantile period. Subsequent development proceeds normally thereafter, but an underlying weakness or immaturity remains within the central nervous system (CNS) which may cause other systems in the body to misfire under certain conditions. The existence and extent of neuro-developmental delay is measured by the presence and the strength of primitive reflexes beyond the normal age of inhibition, and the absence of postural reflexes. The latter should have developed to allow the individual to manipulate and interact effectively within the environment. These aberrant reflexes provide signposts of central nervous system (CNS) maturity.

During normal development, the primitive reflexes should start to emerge, strengthen, fulfill a function, and then undergo inhibition throughout the first year of life. There should be a strict chronology, sequence, and rhythm to this reflex structure, so that by a certain age specific milestones should have been achieved. Should the sequence be interrupted in any way it will result in the early reflexes remaining locked in the system, so that the emergence of subsequent reflexes is disturbed, and further central nervous system development will be built upon eccentric foundations.

The earliest known reflexes to emerge are those that appear at 5-7 weeks after conception and which form a group of "withdrawal reflexes". These represent the earliest observed realization of tactile awareness in the embryo who, when barely visible to the naked eye, will respond to tactile stimulation in the mouth region with a rapid amebiclike withdrawal movement of the whole organism. It has been suggested (Goddard, 1989) that the early withdrawal reflex may be a manifestation of the fear paralysis reflex (FPR) described in detail by Kaada (1986), and which can have important implications in later life if it does not undergo inhibition during the gestational period.

Capute (1986) divides the primitive reflexes into three categories:
1.   Intrauterine reflexes that appear and are suppressed during intrauterine development, (not present at birth).
2.   Intrauterine/Birth reflexes
       Reflexes that appear during later intrauterine development, are present at birth. and are inhibited by 6 months of age.
3.   Postural reflexes
       Reflexes that appear during late infancy following inhibition of the primitive reflexes.

The withdrawal reflexes belong to the first category and should be inhibited at the time of the emergence of the Moro reflex at 9-32 weeks after conception. This suggests that the Moro reflex itself plays an inhibitory role for the preceding reflex, and it is only the development of a full and strong Moro reflex which will complete this task. If the Moro reflex fails to develop .fully during this period, then both the withdrawal reflexes and the Moro reflex will remain "locked" and active in the system beyond the normal age of inhibition.

How can the presence of these two reflexes impair later functioning—and particularly the mechanisms of speech—if they remain active at the subcortical level beyond the age of inhibition?

Kaada (1986) described the characteristics of the fear paralysis reflex using the analogy of the"terrified rabbit", who becomes frozen to the spot at which he has first experienced sudden fear. In the animal kingdom it may serve a useful purpose where the motionless animal will not attract the attention of its predator. Within mankind, it represents a maladaptive response to situations with which the individual is unable to cope.

Its accompanying characteristics are also of significance: Activation of the fear paralysis reflex results in immediate motor paralysis accompanied by respiratory arrest in expiration. Muscle tone is reduced and there is lack of response to external stimuli. A pain suppressing mechanism is released, together with bradycardia and peripheral vasoconstriction. Kaada states that it is "a reflex present in the entire animal kingdom which is temporarily released from cortical control as a result of extreme fear." If it fails to undergo full inhibition at the correct time in humans. then it remains active at the subcortical level, lowering the threshold of fear in the individual, so that it can be activated by minor stimuli, which present no actual threat to the individual at all.

The Moro reflex should emerge from 9-32 weeks after conception, be fully present at birth, and undergo inhibition at 3-4 months of neonate life. At 9-12 weeks other vital systems in the body are also developing: the vestibular system, the cerebellum and the hypothalamus. If the Moro reflex, which is the fetus' primitive alerting mechanism to stress or threat, does not develop fully at this time, it is possible that the fetus' stress responses may be inadequate. For example, (Odent 1986) describes how the entire hormonal profile for later life is regulated during this dynamic period of development.

"At an early stage of fetal life the pituitary gland which controls all other endocrine glands can secrete all the known pituitary hormones. When the fetus is 11-12 weeks old, the vessels that will become the hypothalamus and the pituitary glands come together. By that time. the hypothalamus is already controlling the pituitary. and by the time the fetus is 3 months old, the day-to-day variations in the stress hormone ACTH are already well established."

Specific hormonal states at an age when the basic adaptive system has not reached maturity may set the hormonal levels for life. For instance, if the fetus, or baby is in constant unalleviated stress, this will result in the release of stress hormones and regulate the hypothalamus in such a way, that the seeds for future conditions such as poor stress tolerance and hypertension are sown.

The hypothalamus acts as a bridge between the brain and the hormonal system —it belongs to both, and it plays a leading role in responses to psychological stress. Together with the limbic lobe it stimulates the pituitary axis, the reticular activating system and the sympathetic arm of the autonomic nervous system —three separate circuits that respond to unfamiliarities and to challenge. Activation of these three circuits leads to the release of the stress hormone ACTH together with other hormones from the brain stem and sympathetic nerves, which result in a rise in heart rate, dilation of the pupils, and increased discharge of the reticular activating system which in turn results in increase in muscle tension, rise in blood pressure and heart rate, and the inhibition of reflex bradycardia. These are all the physical symptoms of the activated Moro reflex, which has sometimes been referred to as the initiator of the "fight or flight" mechanism. The Moro may also be regarded as the "release" mechanism from an activated fear paralysis reflex.

What might be the result of both the fear paralysis reflex (FPR) and the Moro reflex remaining active at the subcortical level in an individual?

We would have a person with a low fear threshold and a low stress

A person who may be hypersensitive to touch, sound, specific frequencies of sound, changes in his visual field, smell and possibly taste as well. He may be able to compensate and overcome his hypersensitivity in many situations, but it will involve conscious "over-riding" of instinctive reflexive responses by the cortex. He will become quickly fatigued, and with the fatigue his ability to compensate will be reduced, so that a reflexive response is more easily elicited. Which particular reflex is elicited will depend upon the circumstances. In certain situations both reflexes will be overcome by conscious control and the individual will react to that situation rationally and effectively. At other times, the situation might provoke the Moro or overreaction response. On another occasion the withdrawal reflexes will claim priority, and the individual will find it impossible to respond at all. Elective mutism may be the result of the latter.

What remains to be answered, however, is this: Why should specific social situations provoke such extreme fear?

Where the fear paralysis reflex (FPR) and the Moro Reflex remain, later reflexes in the hierarchical structure will also be aberrant to some degree. The tonic labyrinthine reflex (TLR) may remain in its residual or retained form, so that any movement of the head forwards or backwards beyond the midline point will result in automatic flexion or extension of the arms and the legs—a response that can only be controlled by conscious muscular effort. In that case, balance in the upright position will never be stable or constant. Furthermore, the labyrinthine and oculo-headrighting reflexes which should be present at 6 months of age will not develop fully. This in turn will affect oculomotor functioning.

The tonic labyrinthine reflex (TLR) also exerts a direct influence upon the labyrinth. The labyrinth is a complex organ for attaining balance, which, by movement of fluid in three orthogonal tubes operates rather like a spirit level (carpenter's level) activating special nerves which send signals to the brain concerning movement of the head. The vestibular apparatus then detects changes of direction and position of the head in space, particularly when the movement starts and stops. Information from the vestibular apparatus is combined with information from other sensory channels. Both prenatally and after birth, the vestibular system controls body image impression, and also kinesthesia (the sensation of bodily movement in space).

The vestibular apparatus is also a filtering point for sound. The ear acts as a collecting organ not only for sound stimuli, but also for those stimuli that are responsible for coordinating the vestibular portion of the labyrinth. (Tomatis, 1980) If, as a result of aberrant reflexes, the vestibular is dealing with conflicting messages from other sensory channels, it may impair its ability to process and relay sound messages to the language processing centers in the cortex. The addition of a tonic labyrinthine reflex (TLR) to a fear paralysis reflex (FPR) and a Moro reflex, imposes a new set of problems on the individual. Balance is rarely under automatic control, oculomotor functioning may be erratic and there may be severe sound discrimination problems, so that the individual suffers from the "cocktail party deafness" phenomenon. A string of words together may sound like a meaningless unit. Individual conversation within a group may be perceived as a conglomerate of jumbled sounds which do not immediately make sense. This condition is sometimes referred to as "auditory delay" or "auditory confusion". Such an individual may have a heightened sensitivity to certain frequencies of sound with a lowered sensitivity to other frequencies, with the result that parts of words are not easily registered, and miscellaneous sounds may intrude more readily on the listener's consciousness. Under these circumstances, the environment becomes a disorientating and bewildering one. Each one of us has known at sometime how unpleasant and frightening it is to he lost in a strange place. The child with a strong tonic labyrinthine reflex (TLR), Moro reflex and fear paralysis reflex (FPR), knows what it is like to be "lost" many times in each waking day. In such situations the FPR is easily elicited.

The vestibular apparatus is also linked to the vagus or the tenth cranial nerve at the level of the medulla. (Blythe, 1990) The vagus nerve contains both sensory and motor fibers. The sensory fibers convey sensitivity to part of the external ear, and carry afferent impulses from the pharynx and the larynx and the internal organs of the thorax and abdomen. The motor fibers and accessory nerves serve the striated muscles of the palate, the larynx and the pharynx. If a child is already overloaded by outside stimuli, his compensatory mechanisms are stretched to capacity, so that there is little energy available for expression. Far too much attention is concentrated upon making sense of conflicting perceptions. The confused vestibular excites the vagus nerve and its impulses to the organs of speech production. Over-action of the vestibular alerts earlier aberrant reflexes. The withdrawal reflexes come into play, and the child cannot talk. The fear paralysis reflex impedes breathing, and affects the muscles for speech, which fall in to a temporary paralysis. The child has the ability to talk—but not in this particular environment. His filtering system for outside stimuli is inadequate. His ability to categorize and discriminate and thus to make sense of his environment is impaired. With this information in mind, the 17 year old girl's descriptions of fear and of breathlessness quoted at the beginning of the paper, start to make sense.

The situation may be further complicated by the presence of one other reflex—the asymmetrical tonic neck reflex (ATNR). Where this persists beyond the normal age of inhibition (6 months of neonate life while awake), several areas of functioning may be impaired. In its primitive form the reflex is elicited as the baby turns its head to one side. The limbs on the side to which the head has turned will extend as the occipital limbs flex. When a child starts to learn fine motor activities such as writing, control of the writing hand will be affected each time that the child turns its head to focus on the writing hand. Hand-eye coordination generally may be immature. Balance may be "thrown" when in the upright position, as any movement of the head in a lateral direction will result in stiffening of the limbs to one side. Smooth eye movements may be affected to the extent that eyes, head and body cannot move independently of one another but can only operate as a unit, so that saccades can only be accomplished with head and/or body tracking. The continued presence of the ATNR will also interfere with the establishment of unilaterality of brain functioning. (Gesell & Ames, 1947) Any task that involves crossing the midline may present difficulties. (Bobath, 1975) A dominant ear and a dominant language center may never have been fully established, so that the child switches erratically from left to right hemisphere for receptive and expressive language tasks.

Both the left and the right hemispheres in the brain have language centers, but the left side is the most efficient for the majority of the population. The left side of the brain is also responsible for the execution of methodical, sequential tasks, while the right side of the brain is responsible for scanning and targeting. If a child has an inadequate filtering mechanism, then the cortex is bombarded by an overload of information which should have been screened earlier in the receiving line. It should have reached the cortex partly categorized, with miscellaneous information filtered out. If this has not occurred, then the left side of the brain will be greatly overworked performing tasks which should have been completed earlier in the receptive process. The processing may then need to switch to the right-brain language center, which the child cannot utilize as immediately or as fluently. The brain may continue switching from righ to left functions. Receiving, processing and the expression of language are not automatic tasks for him in any situation which involves too many stimuli. This child reaches overload far too quickly. With overload comes confusion: confusion generates fear, so that the FPR (fear paralysis reflex) may be activated, and once again the child is unable to speak.

If we return to the earlier DSM III definition of elective mutism, the interpretation may be rather different in the light of these reflexes: "Refusal to speak" may be seen as "inability to speak" and "including at school" may be replaced by "specially at school," where the child does not perceive the environment to be a safe one, because he cannot make sense of it. On the other hand, his willingness to communicate via gestures and nodding starts to seem perfectly reasonable. The associated features also warrant further examination. FPR would induce excessive shyness, social isolation and withdrawal, together with a fear of school. Compulsive traits and negativism tend to be an attempt to establish order and security in an insecure and frightening world. Albeit these are self-defeating strategies for the individual in that situation, they provide some temporary reassurance of self-control in a world that has no safe framework for them in which they could operate effectively. Both DSM III's and DSM IV's apparently incongruous listing of "temper tantrums" as another symptom, presents possibly further manifestation—the second half of the puzzle: a sensory overload comes far too fast for this kind of child.

Fear paralysis reflex invokes a state of withdrawal and temporary paralysis. The Moro reflex, on the other hand, elicits an over-reactive response to certain stimuli. Where the fear paralysis reflex remains active in the system at the subcortical level, the Moro reflex will also remain active. (If it does not, then there is no "safety mechanism" to "arouse" the individual from the fear paralysis reflex and in extreme cases, death will result. Sudden infant death syndrome (SIDS) may be one example of this.) Children who have disappeared into the withdrawal state, may only emerge from that state either with a violent outburst of anger, tears of frustration or with hyperactivity. If, finally, the Moro reflex is activated it "releases" them from their paralyzed state. These children are the product of an unresolved conflict between two opposing reflexes, which should not even be present beyond the age of 4 months of neonate life.

Other forms of elective mutism may also be part of this conflict. The individual is unable to verbalize feelings, or to recount events which have a traumatic content. The associated feelings or sensations are so great that the individual becomes imprisoned in a silence which both locks in the feeling and forms part of the pathway to shock. One 11 year old girl later asked: "Why couldn't you see that the way I was, was telling you what I was saying?" as if the silence spoke more loudly and more eloquently than any words could have. In such situations, it is as if the "fight or flight" mechanism is activated, but cannot be released. The fear paralysis traps those sensations inside, before the "fight or flight" mechanism can be used and the internal excitation dispersed. Constant repetition of an "emergency" situation without the ability to fight it, or to run away from it, may result in states of extreme withdrawal (helplessness) and depression, as the activated feelings are turned inward but will not go away. Individuals of this type will find most forms of therapy extremely threatening, as the only release mechanism they know is an explosive and cataclysmic one which they constantly fight to control.

Blythe (1971, 1976) found that the true emotional regressive phase of the hypnotic state would be interrupted if speech was introduced, and the subject was expected to talk during regression. It was as if in the process of speech, the patient lost contact with the feelings. Elective mutism would appear to be the opposite side of the same coin, i.e. where bodily and perceptual sensation is too great, the pathway to speech becomes strangled.

The Institute for Neuro-Physiological Psychology has achieved improvement with a small number of elective mutes on a reflex inhibition program. Initially, the aim has been to stimulate an existing Moro reflex until it is present in its fully retained form. This gives the child a second chance to utilize the Moro reflex—both as an inhibitor to its predecessor, the fear paralysis reflex (FPR) and to give the child the full release mechanisms that it may never have had at any previous stage in its life. Paradoxically, as the Moro reflex reaches its fully retained form, many of the symptoms of overreactivity and oversensitivity actually abate, as if, at last, the body can utilize its instinctive channels of response to danger, to the full.

Brunnstrom (1962, 1970) may provide one explanation for this. She worked as a physical therapist promoting mobility in children and adults with severe cerebral palsy. She provoked primitive movement patterns which she had observed to be present following either pyramidal tract damage or which are present normally in the fetus. She stated that: *"A patient may be able to perform voluntary flexor and extensor movements, only by utilizing the facilitating effect of one or the other of these reflexes. When a conflict between will and inhibitory reflex impulse exists, the will does not always gain supremacy."*

Finally, the majority of these children have marked vestibular problems.

Vestibular stimulation would seem to be an obvious starting point for a rehabilitation or remediation program. However, as was observed when doing the program as designed at the Institute for Neuro-Physiological Psychology, occupational therapists using the A. Jean Ayres' sensory motor training program, have found that a number of the children who require vestibular stimulation either cannot tolerate it, or only benefit from it to a limited degree. Where the fear paralysis reflex and Moro reflexes are still present, vestibular stimulation may activate one or both of these, so that the patient either finds it too distressing or it reinforces faulty existing compensatory strategies. There may be improvement in gross muscle coordination and balance, but there is rarely a spillover into educational performance. If, however, vestibular stimulation is added <u>after</u> the FPR and Moro reflex have undergone inhibition, the individual is less sensitive, and the program is far more effective, and there will be concomitant improvement in educational performance.

All of the above suggests that there is a physical basis for elective mutism. While accepting that there are cases of both elective mutism and traumatic mutism which are the result of psychological factors, it is nevertheless maintained that for the majority, the psychological factors are of a secondary nature. Where both a fear paralysis reflex (FPR) and a Moro reflex remain active in the individual, certain social situations will present extreme threat. Extreme threat will engender vulnerability in the susceptible individual. Such vulnerability will be accompanied by fear —fear may activate early primitive reflexes at any time in the case of "elective mutism"—paralyzing the organs of speech in specific situations.

DEVELOPMENTAL MILESTONES:
A BLUEPRINT FOR SURVIVAL

SALLY GODDARD N.D.T.

Presented to the Institute for Neuro-Physiological Psychology, November, 1990.

The milestones of life may have been set for us long before we make our entry into the world, but each one should herald our safe arrival from the previous stage of our life, so that we build each stage, block upon solid block. Not everyone is fortunate enough to achieve each milestone. A small percentage will not survive pregnancy. Another percentage will find the process of birth too arduous a journey, and will die during the birth process or shortly afterwards. Another percentage will survive birth and the first hazardous days of life, but may already have had to struggle from conception through pregnancy and birth. They arrive in the world "normal" to all appearances, but with weaknesses in the system which make them vulnerable to a host of minor stressors. It is for this group that each milestone of life may present a threat, or, as Blythe in a 1987 lecture has suggested, it may highlight the basic faults in the system which leave the individual prone to a range of conditions, from sudden infant death syndrome (SIDS) to an inability to cope with stress in later life.

It is upon this specific group that this paper will focus, as it is maintained that their symptoms stem directly from an immaturity in the central nervous system (CNS)and the associated nerve tracts, and its interaction with other systems in the body. Substantiation of this statement will involve the more detailed examination of three systems:
 The Reflex System
 The Vestibular Apparatus
 The Reticular Formation

Every child born into the world should be born with a set of reflexes which are for the infant's survival, and which form the basic reflex system. They start to emerge in utero and should be inhibited, or in certain cases transformed, by a higher part of the brain during pregnancy and the first year of neonate life. If this fails to occur, then they remain aberrant, and they represent a structural weakness in the central nervous system (CNS). The emergence and inhibition of reflexes at the correct time plays a vital role in myelination of the nerves, and it is upon this, that the resulting human being will eventually depend for its efficient functioning at all levels of consciousness.

From the moment of conception the "neural clock" starts to tick, and should continue to do so throughout life. For some people, the clock slips out of kilter very early in development. Though they appear to "make up" the loss and progress through life normally, their ability to function easily and fluently in specific areas may be impaired. The brain and body do not always work in perfect unison. The dysfunction may be barely detectable so that strategies can be used to overcome the problem, but as the stressors become greater, so the compensatory mechanisms start to break down, and the weakness manifests itself. It may appear first in the nursery, the classroom, the playground, or the sportsfield. Often it does not appear until much later, when the adult becomes involved in the more complex processes of life such as career, childbirth, stress and the general demands of modern living. As growing up continues, so more and more systems become involved in a mismatched system of communication. For example: The central nervous system (CNS) may direct incorrect messages to the hypothalamus and the pituitary system, which in turn then—wrongly— influence hormone activity, hunger and satiety, temperature control, libido, and emotions, to name but a few. The reflex structure provides the incorrect blueprint for a complex network of wiring and contacts from one system in the body to another.

The etiology of this syndrome which The Institute for Neuro-Physiological Psychology (INPP) in Chester has termed neuro-developmental delay, is diverse and frequently indeterminate, but it has been suggested that the symptoms which range from clumsiness and ambidexterity, to learning difficulties and emotional disorder, may be hereditary in origin in 50% of the cases, extending back as far as four generations. Eustis (1947) suggested that it is "...characterized by a slow rate of neuromuscular maturation, implying retarded myelination of the motor and associated nerve tracts." Subsequent events may then take their toll, as antenatal problems, difficult birth and injury or illness during the first year of life may instigate or reinforce a preexisting weakness of the central nervous system(CNS). Each system interacting with it then misfires with varying degrees of deviation.

Let us examine how the reflex system provides such a base:
The process of normal development is dependent upon the emergence, inhibition and in certain instances, transformation of these primitive reflexes, so that postural reflexes may be released preparing a child for progressive development. "the nervous system learns by doing."(Gilfoyle, Grady & Moore) and reflexive action aids the continued opening up of neural pathways. Motor behavior should be the product of a system in which brain and body work together to form a communicating system of response, action and expression.

Messages should be transmitted with equal efficiency from brain to body and back again, via the efferent and afferent systems. If this is disrupted in any way, then subsequent motor and sensory functions may be affected, altering the transmission of messages from one system in the body to another, and further distorting perceptions, and their transposition from sensory experience into thought, language, emotion, and even the ability to deal with that sensory experience itself.

It is as if the processing or filtering system in the brain cannot cope with a plethora of information, and therefore "cuts out" at a very crude level. It is bombarded by conflicting sensory stimuli which it cannot categorize immediately, and it becomes overloaded far too quickly.

The first area of sensory response to develop in utero is the tactile response, and its realization may be observed in the primitive withdrawal reflex which first appears between 5 and 7 weeks after conception. Early avoidance reflexes —and Gilfoyle, Grady & Moore state that there are many of them in the first few weeks of uterine life— form the basis of the developing reflex structure. Capute (1986) says that these very early reflexes emerge in utero and should be inhibited in utero: that they should have been controlled by higher centers in the fetal development system before later reflexes in utero can develop fully.

At 9 weeks after conception, as the withdrawal reflexes are being controlled, the Moro reflex should start to emerge. Both the vestibular system and the cerebellum are also developing at this time. Let us suppose, that at this dynamic stage in development, either as a result of faulty genetic programming, or some current uterine or external anomaly, something shifts imperceptibly out of phase. The avoidance reflexes remain active in the chain instead of being inhibited by the developing Moro reflex at 9-12 weeks gestation. The Moro reflex itself then fails to develop fully. Subsequent reflexes emerge, and fulfill their function to a degree, but they remain "locked" in the system, neither fully aiding the embryo through each stage in development, nor undergoing full inhibition at the appropriate time.

Because they may not persist in a retained form, they remain undetected, and the resulting person is deemed medically to be "normal". There is a basic weakness in the system, however, which will exact a price later at the conscious level, for the tasks which should be automatic, have not become so.

The reflex system is built in a sequence with each reflex playing both a facilitatory and an inhibitory role in the reflex chain. The Landau reflex, for example, aids inhibition of the tonic labyrinthine reflex (TLR), and Capute has suggested that the symmetrical tonic neck reflex (STNR) may be a part of the process of the tonic labyrinthine (TLR) undergoing transformation. Thus, a correct sequence from the beginning is a vital precursor to the development of the central nervous system, as well as motor, perceptual, cognitive and emotional development. Each reflex affects a specific area of functioning. Different combinations of aberrant reflexes will build different pictures, different problems and different people.

The question that poses itself here is: How can three of the earliest reflexes impair later functioning and affect other systems in the body if they remain "locked" in the chain?

The withdrawal reflex which, first appears at 5-7 weeks after conception, is initially a rapid amebic-like withdrawal movement of the whole organism as a response to touch in the oral region. A few days later the head will turn away from the stimulus, and by the end of the 12th week the eyes will close—tightly shut—as an additional response.

It has been suggested (Goddard, 1989), that these early withdrawal reflexes may be the earliest manifestation of a fear paralysis reflex (FPR), described in detail by Kaada (1986), as a major factor in sudden infant death syndrome (SIDS). He describes many of its characteristics in infancy, where it may be recognized as the "terrified rabbit", who becomes frozen to the spot at which he has first experienced sudden fear. Kaada describes its features, beginning with an immediate motor paralysis accompanied by respiratory arrest in expiration, reduced muscle tone, lack of response to external stimuli, activation of a pain-suppressing mechanism and bradycardia with peripheral vasoconstriction. It may be accompanied by an increase in systolic pressure and pulse pressure combined with muscle hypotonia. It represents a maladaptive response to situations with which the individual is unable to cope.

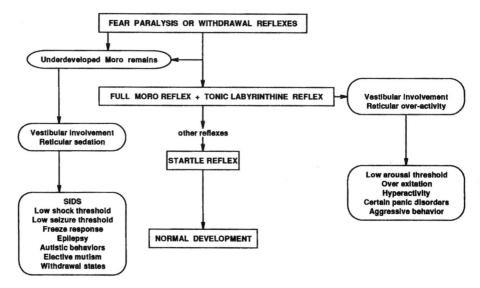

The Moro reflex has been described as the "first primitive shock response." (Bennett, 1988) It should be inhibited by three months of neonate life, and then transformed into the adult startle reflex or Strauss reflex. It has also been described as the initiator of the "fight or flight" mechanism as its activation stimulates the sympathetic nervous system in preparation for what it interprets to be a life threatening event. The Moro reflex demands instant reflexive response, irrespective of the source of real or imagined danger. Bennett suggested that its continued presence beyond three months of neonate life, is a major factor in anxiety states, as the individual remains hypersensitive to minor stimuli and the Moro demands an overreactive response. Here, the limbic system switches to "emergency" before the cortex has time to filter out the source of distress and to direct a rational response.

In the neonate, the Moro reflex appears as a violent, distressed reflex. Arms and legs will convulsively extend, freeze fractionally, and then abduct. As the limbs go out, the head will be thrown back and there will be a massive intake of breath in preparation for the lifesaving scream.

If this reflex persists beyond three to four months of neonate life, it will result in a degree of hypersensitivity and over reactivity, depending upon its strength. If it is only residually present in those first few months of life, the implications may be rather different. The reflex may be weak in its entirety, or, the second part of the reflex may be underdeveloped or even absent. In that case, although there may be a massive intake of breath, the ensuing abduction of the arms and the releasing of the breath cannot take place. This would result in respiratory arrest in expiration so that breathing appears to "freeze" and the baby's cry for help is never uttered. The baby becomes captured in the "freeze" state —the possible remnant of the fear paralysis reflex (FPR). It is not dissimilar to the experience of "dry drowning", which can occur if someone is thrown unexpectedly into extremely cold water. Everything in the body "locks" from the shock of the cold, so that it is impossible to expand or contract the lungs —either to inhale or to exhale breath. Within a very short time it is possible to drown in this way, without any water ever entering the lungs.

Cottrell (1987) became interested in a correlation between asthma and the continued presence of the Moro reflex. He stated: "All primitive reflexes require a compensation mechanism from higher centers of the brain. The Moro, being a startle reflex, requires an overriding effect. The adult version of the "fight or flight" response is more sophisticated and will, whenever possible, be given priority by the body. This requires several differing types of compensations. First, is the necessity to restore the normal mechanism of controlling the muscular reaction. Second, is the need to produce adrenaline reaction to any frightening situation. This is done through lowering the stimulus threshold, which makes for a very frightened individual who is hypersensitive and overresponds to every threat."

"Where there is a retained or residual Moro, the CO_2 reflex does not develop. The combination between that lack of CO_2 and the need to keep the individual from taking that deep breath, leads to shallow apical breathing, and frequently to hyperventilation —an important precursor to panic."

Cottrell's observations touch on three important areas: respiratory functioning, rigid control of muscle tone and adrenal output. Each one of these may play a vital instigating and/or a sustaining role in panic disorders and a range of other conditions for which there appears to be no adequate pathology, and which are therefore regarded as "psychosomatic illnesses". Gold (1986), described one aspect of this: "When the child's cortex gets into overload, it sends messages to the adrenal gland and the pituitary. All they can tell is that they got a signal to squirt out their chemicals. Each time, when they get the signal the adrenals squirt out adrenaline and cortisol. Pretty soon the adrenals get exhausted. As the adrenals get exhausted, allergies start to show up along with psychosomatic illnesses, headaches, migraines, colitis ulcers and high blood pressure. Hay Fever is one of the symptoms."

Odent (1984) describes part of this syndrome another way. He outlines Laborit's (1952) concept of "inhibition of action", a term used to describe a basically submissive behavioral pattern. This is a direct result of an inability to respond to a stressful situation by either fight or flight. In experiments on rats, Laborit was able to trace the origin of high blood pressure to just such situations of continuous frustration.

Odent's hormonal studies confirm Laborit's theory: "Inhibition of action generates the secretion of noradrenaline and cortisol; cortisol itself triggers the inhibition of action the result being a vicious circle ... noradrenaline contracts the blood vessels, quickens the heartbeat, and raises the blood pressure, and cortisol has many kinds of long term effects, such as depressing the immune system and destroying the thymus."

Odent links continuous hormonal reactions to pathogenic situations of this kind, as major factors in the etiology of psychosomatic diseases. It is therefore of interest that both the withdrawal reflexes and the Moro reflex exert a direct influence upon these reaction patterns.

The third reflex I would like to look at, which takes a leading role in the interplay between the systems in the body, is the tonic labyrinthine reflex (TLR). It is thought that this reflex also emerges in recognizable form towards the end of the first trimester of pregnancy. Capute (1986), suggests that flexus habitus itself may be a manifestation of the TLR forwards, but the TLR backwards may not be fully activated for the first time until the baby's head goes into extension before entering the birth canal. (Machover, 1990) This may be one reason why the full reflex in both flexion and extension is generally not accepted to be present until after birth. The tonic labyrinthine reflex (TLR) is the infant's only way of reacting to gravity, and is normally present in its crude form by 3 months of neonate life. If the baby is lying on its back with the trunk supported, then the reflex may be elicited by allowing the head to drop back below the midline. This will result in an extensor thrust of the arms and the legs. If the head is then brought forward above the midline, the baby will start to curl up into a fetal position. If the reflex is still active when the baby makes the transition to toddler, then the head righting reflexes, which are essential to sit and to stand, will be impaired and the balance will be affected when in the upright position. Any movement of the head too far forwards or backwards will result in either reflexive flexion or reflexive extension of the limbs. Only through conscious muscular effort and in direct conflict with the reflexive response, can these movements be controlled.

What happens if we try to act in direct opposition to a normal reflexive response? Imagine that you have touched a scalding kettle. The immediate natural reaction is to withdraw the hand as quickly as possible. If you deliberately act against this reflex, what happens? The obvious result is that the hand gets burned, but what are the other reactions in the body? There is a change in breathing, increase in heart rate, and tightening of all the muscles in the body as the body "armors" itself against the natural reaction. When at last you do "give way" to the reflex there is relief, a feeling of fatigue and probably little knowledge of what else has occurred in the immediate environment during the period of time that you have been fighting the reflex. Individuals with a cluster of aberrant reflexes have to perform this ritual in every moment of their waking lives in order to function normally. In extreme, there is a choice of only two directions to cope: Either hyperactivity, as a means of keeping the system "on the go", or withdrawal, in one or several areas of life, so that the most difficult or sensitive situations can be avoided.

The tonic labyrinthine reflex also exerts a direct influence upon the labyrinth. The labyrinth is a complex organ for attaining balance, which, by movement of fluid in three orthogonal tubes operates rather like a spirit level, activating special nerves which send signals to the brain concerning movement of the head. The vestibular apparatus then detects changes of direction and position of the head in space, particularly when the movement starts and stops. It also records the amount of forwards, backwards or sideways tilting of the head, as well as its movement when the whole body moves in a linear direction. Odent suggests that it is the vestibular organ which directs the fetus' orientation in utero, and deficiencies in its function might result in breech or shoulder presentations at birth. Information from the vestibular apparatus is combined with information from other sensory channels. Both pre-natally and post-natally the vestibular system controls bodyimage impression and reinforcement, and also kinesthesia—the sensation of bodily movement in space. If a strong tonic labyrinthine reflex (TLR) persists, then balance will be constantly "thrown". Messages received by the vestibular will be inaccurate and fluctuating. The cortex will have to perform a detective task in decoding which messages are relevant and which are irrelevant.

One example of the cortex at work can be seen in cases of auditory delay, or auditory confusion. The ear acts as a collecting organ not only for sound stimuli, but also for those stimuli that are responsible for coordinating the vestibular portion of the labyrinth. (Tomatis 1980) If the vestibular, as a result of aberrant reflexes, is receiving conflicting messages from other sensory channels, its processing may be impaired. The confusion may make it unable to relay sound messages received from the ear to the language processing centers in the cortex. Another example may be seen in some autistic children, who fail to respond to communication through the auditory channel, although there is no evidence of hearing loss. These children may already be in such a state of internal excitation and arousal that, to cope at all, they have to amputate one system from their consciousness.

Activation of the tonic labyrinthine reflex (TLR) involves both the vestibular apparatus and the reticular formation. The reticular formation is net-like in appearance and is situated in the central part of the brain stem. It operates as the basis of an alerting system, by sending messages to the cerebral cortex and the afferent pathways, in order to maintain the brain in a condition in which consciousness can occur. The ascending pathways have an arousing function, while the descending pathways—via the reticulospinal tract—influence the neuron pools. The facilitatory area fires spontaneously, but the inhibitory area (which has a sedating affect), relies on the basal ganglia, cerebellum and cortex. It is stated in Merck (1987) that: "the alert state requires an instant interaction between the cognitive functions of the cerebral hemispheres and the arousal mechanisms of the reticular formation."

If the reticular formation fails to act appropriately, then unconsciousness can be the result. Within the reticular formation are areas which regulate the cardiovascular, respiratory, endocrine and gastrointestinal systems. Emotions also come under its influence through the limbic system and hypothalamus. Brain (1987), suggests that epilepsy may be one result of a misfiring in the reticular formation, the origins stemming back to an immaturity within the central nervous system (CNS), which lowers the threshold to seizure.

In the light of this, it may be possible to devise a schema, whereby a misfiring in the brain stem as a direct result of aberrant reflexes results in either extreme over-excitation (hyperactivity), or under-stimulation (the cutting out of one or more sensory channels until eventual total unconsciousness is the outcome) i.e. the filtering mechanism is not doing its job. Instead of sifting and dumping irrelevant information and stimuli, it allows everything to pass through to higher centers in the brain. This would either heighten arousal to an abnormal level, or it would close the gate entirely, so that the system goes into "shut down".

In what circumstances might this "shut down" operate? Epilepsy may be one, where the threshold to seizure is low as a result of immaturity within the central nervous system. Fay (1942) even went so far as to describe an epileptic fit as, "a defense reflex" which attempts by convulsive efforts to regain a favorable formula or a state of equilibrium. There are, of course, varying types and degrees of seizure, not all of which can be categorized as "epileptic". At this point I would like to look further at how "seizure-like" episodes may stem from withdrawal reflexes remaining active in the nervous system chain. The result would be an inadequate interaction between the vestibular apparatus, reticular activating system and cerebellum, with subsequent impairment to the arousal mechanisms.

Southall, Samuels & Talbert (1990), have recently produced a study on the incidence of cyanotic episodes in potential sudden infant death syndrome (SIDS) babies and those who actually became SIDS victims. Many of the symptoms they describe bear a remarkable resemblance to the features of the fear paralysis reflex (FPR), (Kaada, 1986), and to the "seizure-like" episodes experienced by adults for which no adequate medical explanation can be found. Tests may have been carried out for a number of conditions such as diabetes, hypoglycemia, epilepsy, thyroid malfunction and even for tumors, with none of these being detected. Southall, Samuels & Talbert, describe cyanotic episodes which occur at a median age of 7 weeks of neonate life, when the Moro reflex should be at its height. They note that the most common trigger was a sudden naturally occurring stimulus from pain, fear or anger, most often in the form of a sudden shock. In their studies they found no evidence of actual seizure activity, but episodes were more common when the infant was tired (reduced ability to compensate for the weakness), when there was a high level of emotional tension in the home, or when the routine of the infant was interrupted. Infection, particularly respiratory infection, increased the frequency and severity of the episodes.

These episodes commonly began with a series of attempts at expiratory cries without inspiratory effort and with a widely open mouth. If crying became established, the attack was unlikely to develop further. If it did not, then within 30 seconds unconsciousness would ensue accompanied either by opisthotonus or tonic convulsion, or both. At the beginning of the episode the heart rate would rise to above 170 beats per minute (B.P.M.) dropping dramatically to around 80 B.P.M. as bradycardia progressed. Now, let us examine how these symptoms may link with Kaada's description of the fear paralysis reflex (FPR) outlined earlier. Kaada describes it as "a reflex present in the entire animal kingdom, which is temporarily released from cortical control as a result of extreme fear." It is accompanied by bradycardia which acts as disinhibitory phenomenon and is the final manifestation of a common pathway to shock. The reflex when activated leaves no trace of itself in the organism, so that no adequate cause can be established for the cessation of breathing and pulmonary effort. If the fear paralysis reflex remains active at the subcortical level, then the Moro reflex cannot operate fully to open the airways, or to allow exhalation in moments of extreme crisis. If this is added to a heightened sensibility to shock, the results may be fatal. Southall, Samuels & Talbert suggest a definite link between brain-stem defects, including disturbances to the respiratory generators, to the centers controlling pulmonary vasomotor tone, and to the processing of reflexes arising in the pulmonary vascular bed or lung. Thus, a misfiring in the brain stem from those reflexes which influence breathing, circulation and arousal may be responsible for a number of behaviors. Lack of adequate arousal may be a result, not of under sensitivity, but of hypersensitivity, where the threshold of tolerance to external stimuli is abnormally low. In such cases, even touching may be painful, and many bodily sensations a torment rather than a reassurance or a pleasure.

Certain autistic behaviors can be linked to sensory input overload of this kind. Many autistic children cannot tolerate wearing clothes, and most of them will remove their shoes and socks whenever possible. Many are excessively ticklish and cannot stand even simple daily routines such as being dried with a towel. Eating may present problems, as they detest either very smooth or very chewy food and may insist on a narrow, repetitive diet. It has been observed (O'Reilly, 1989) that they appear to be more responsive after vigorous exercise, and some of their autistic symptoms lessen during episodes of diarrhea and vomiting, prolonged fasting, or —if they are epileptic— after an epileptic episode. It is as if they attempt to raise, artificially, the arousal mechanisms which they need to function, and to maintain their performance at a more alert level. Both exercise and fasting have long been recognized as producing mild states of euphoria. Vomiting and diarrhea alter the body chemistry, leaving a heightened concentration of insulin active in the system, as the body normally produces insulin in response to any intake of food. Under normal conditions, food is consumed and converted into glucose which is utilized by the body for energy, and gradually the blood glucose level drops. Where excessive exercise has taken place, or bouts of vomiting or diarrhea have occurred, there will be too great a concentration of insulin left in the blood, as the blood glucose level will drop much faster. Lowering of the blood glucose level stimulates the secretions of the adrenal glands whose hormones have the opposite effect to insulin. These hormones are passed in the blood to the liver, where they facilitate the conversion of stored glycogen into glucose, balancing the action of insulin so that in normal health an optimum blood sugar level is maintained. Adrenaline secreted by the adrenal center should produce a similar "balancing" effect, but its rate of use is rather different. It forms part of the emergency system which stimulates a rapid glucose increase to provide a sudden energy surge, but which also plunges the individual into a state of hyper-awareness and hyper-responsiveness a state of artificially induced hormonal arousal. Certain cases of anorexia and bulimia may also be part of this vicious cycle. Stress alone can cause dramatic fluctuations in blood sugar level as emotional aggravation induces a rise in blood sugar to deal with the immediate crisis. The rise in blood sugar is then countered by increased insulin secretion with a subsequent fall in blood sugar—another vicious cycle is set in motion.

At its most extreme, the continued presence of the withdrawal reflexes may result in death or unconsciousness, but other permutations are also possible. The withdrawal reflexes may remain active in the chain at the suppressed level. The Moro reflex develops and functions normally for a percentage of the time, but does not always have an over-riding effect over the withdrawal reflexes. Both remain active in the system beyond the normal age of inhibition, performing a juggling feat as to which exerts priority. In certain instances both reflexes will be overcome by conscious control, and the individual will respond to a situation rationally and effectively. At other times, (frequently when the individual is tired), the situation may provoke the Moro reflex, and an over-reaction response. On another occasion the withdrawal reflexes will claim priority, and the individual my find it impossible to respond at all. One example of this interplay between control and the reflexes, may be seen in cases of so-called elective mutism. A child may be loquacious and articulate in one environment, (usually the home environment), but when placed in a less familiar or less secure setting will refuse to respond verbally to any form of communication. Both the terms "elective mutism" and "refuse to respond" infer that the child chooses to remain silent on these occasions. What is far more probable, is that the child cannot speak in these settings.

Let us take a hypothetical case, and examine how a reflex profile might impair the mechanisms of speech under certain conditions: A child reaches the age of 7 with a reflex profile as follows: a residually present Moro reflex, a residually present asymmetrical tonic neck reflex and a virtually retained tonic labyrinthine reflex. He is hypersensitive to sound and to touch. His balance is unstable, his head righting reflexes are under-developed, and thus his spatial awareness and orientation skills are poor. He is stimulus bound, and his eyes do not always work as they should.

Each day, when he goes to school, he walks into an environment which, at best, is buzzing with noise, movement and activity. At its worst, it is a conglomerate of individual sounds which ebb and flow from continuous background noise. He cannot discriminate, categorize and occlude miscellaneous noise or movement immediately, because he does not have an automatic filtering mechanism for the auditory, visual or proprioceptive channels. He has either to attend to outside stimuli or to dismiss them through a conscious and methodical route. Both the left and the right hemispheres, in the brain, have language centers, but the most efficient is on the left side for the majority of the population. It is the left side of the brain which is responsible for the execution of methodical, sequential tasks, while the right side of the brain is responsible for scanning and targeting. For example, if you were seeking out a face in a crowd, the left brain would go through every face in the crowd in order, until it found the one it was looking for. The right brain would scan the faces until it hit on its target. For children without an adequate filtering mechanism, the left brain is being greatly overworked, and they may need to switch to the right brain (subdominant) language center which they cannot utilize as fluently. The environment of noise and strange place is, therefore, a very frightening one for this child.

The vestibular apparatus is constantly monitoring, adjusting and correcting. It is also linked to the l0th or vagus nerve at the level of the medulla (Blythe, 1990). This vagus nerve contains two sets of fibers.

1. Sensory fibers which carry messages to part of the external ear, and afferent messages from the pharynx, larynx and thoracic and abdominal viscera.

2. Motor fibers and accessory nerves, which serve the striated muscles of the palate, larynx and pharynx.

This child is already overloaded by stimuli, and his compensatory mechanisms are stretched to capacity. Too much energy is taken up in attempting to regulate incoming stimuli, and he has little left for expression. The overworked vestibular excites the vagus nerve and its impulses to the organs of speech production. Overreaction of the vestibular also alerts earlier aberrant reflexes. Now the withdrawal reflexes come into play, and he cannot talk. In order to function at all in other areas, speech is eliminated entirely, until either he reaches an environment in which he can relax his controls, or, until the level of overload becomes so great that the Moro is activated, releasing an explosive expressive reaction.

A similar reaction pattern may be seen in cases of emotional stress where the individual is unable to verbalize feelings, or to recount events which have a traumatic content. The associated feelings are so great, that the individual becomes imprisoned in a state of emotional mutism or hysterical paralysis, as part of the pathway to shock. The words of expression may be frantically circulating inside the head, but the feelings are so overwhelming that the person cannot release the mechanisms to speech. One 11 year old girl asked later, when her problems had been resolved, "Why couldn't you see that the way I was, was telling you what I was saying?" A burst of anger, or a flood of tears may open the gateway to speech, as the Moro is finally activated, to release from the partly paralyzed state.

Hypersensitivity with a lowered threshold to shock was suggested as one pathway. The overloaded system goes into "shutdown" in one or more sensory channels in order to cope. The other pathway outlined was that resulting from a lowered arousal threshold, which catapults the system into an increasing state of arousal and over-activity.

Where there is arousal, internal excitation and muscle tension increase.

Where there is prolonged muscle tension, eventually there is fatigue. Fatigue will reduce performance, so that in order to maintain the same level of performance and make up the loss of efficiency, there will need to be an increased level of arousal. Thus, a vicious circle is created, in which over-activity of body musculature becomes both a survival and a performance system. Tiredness becomes an enemy to be overcome, not by rest and restoration, but by increased movement and activity like changing gear up, as the revs increase. A crisis is reached when after topgear and overdrive, there are no further gears to change up to, but somehow the same level of performance has to be maintained. This may be achieved temporarily by boosting adrenaline in the system, whether it be through drugs, more excitement, or by violent outbursts in the form of anger, extreme depression or states of elation. These individuals may be hypersensitive to drugs and to alcohol, to the extent that the drugs actually have the opposite effect to the normal one.

It has been recognized for a number of years that certain hyperactive children react badly to mild sedatives such as Phenergan (Avomine) and Vallergan. Far from calming them down, these drugs will throw them into a state of heightened aggression and distress. These children need their constant activity to keep them going. Momentum and movement are means of survival— by sedating these, you take away the only way they know of functioning. If given a stimulant such as Ritalin (Dextroamphetamine) you actually help them to perform to their level, without the constant need for self induced overarousal.

It has been found in a number of cases by the Institute for Neuro-Physiological Psychology, that if you increase the Moro until it is present for a short time in its fully retained form, many of the symptoms of fatigue and over-excitation actually diminish. It is as if, by allowing the subject to use the primitive "fight or flight" mechanism to its fullest, the internal tension and excitation is released, until the primitive Moro reflex is no longer required by the body and, together with other reflex abnormalities, the Moro can undergo transformation. As greater automatic control is achieved within the body, so many of the presenting symptoms remiss.

To summarize: Analysis of the reflex system provides signposts to the functioning of the central nervous system (CNS) as the reflexes provide the foundation for a mature CNS, which then interlinks with all other systems in the body.

It is here suggested that early damage to the Reflex Sequence may lead to dysfunctions in the Vestibular Apparatus and the Reticular Formation, resulting in either over-sedation (as in Sudden Infant Death Syndrome, Epilepsy, seizure-like episodes, and certain autistic behaviors) or at the other extreme, over-arousal, where certain panic disorders or "neurotic" states may be the outcome.

WHY DO OUR CHILDREN ROLL AND TUMBLE?

By Sally Goddard

Published in "First Steps" magazine, Australia.

The first of all the senses to develop, is the sense of balance. It is vital for posture, movement, and a sense of "center" in space, time, motion, depth and self. All other sensation passes through the balance mechanism (vestibular system) at brain stem level before it is passed on to its specialized region higher in the brain. Hence, all the other senses which a child will depend upon for learning are linked to balance.

To the newborn baby, perception and motion are the same thing. He is not aware that sound and movement, vision and touch are separate sensations, as for him they all fuse together as a single experience or feeling. Thus motion is the child's first language, and the more eloquent he becomes in his primary language, the quicker he will develop other powers of expression, exploration and development.

Stimulation of the balance mechanism is an integral part of the embryo's growth from the moment of conception. Every movement that the mother makes is felt in the cushioned environment of the womb. After birth the feelings continue to be sensed through a vast repertoire of movement patterns from lying, kicking, rolling and sitting, to crawling and creeping on the hands and knees, walking, running hopping, skipping, swinging, rolling and tumbling. It is through movement that further connections are made between the vestibular apparatus and higher centers of the brain. It takes until the age of 7 - 8 years for the balance mechanism, the cerebellum and the corpus callosum to be myelinated, and it is during these early years that vestibular stimulation is the natural ingredient in every normal child's play.

The infant begins with constant repetition of arm and leg movements, practicing extension and flexion of the muscles and training hand-eye coordination. The 8 month old child who rolls back and forth across the floor with no particular goal in sight, is preparing her balance for sitting, standing and eventually walking. As far as she is concerned, when she moves, the world moves with her, and when she stops the world stands still once more. Creeping on hands and knees then acts as an important bridge, enabling her to combine the use of her vestibular, proprioceptive and visual systems for the first time. Walking then increases not only mobility, but allows her to roam with independent use of the hands. These are the early building blocks for learning which must then be practiced and integrated with other systems. Thus, in the early years, movement is the child's main vocabulary and language is body based. Voluntary control of movement can only develop though the broadening of movement horizons.

The 3 - 6 year old child who constantly hops, skips and twirls while "walking" down the street, is still learning to control her balance, for the most advanced level of balance is the ability stay still. The action of NOT moving requires whole body functions and muscle groups to operate together without continuous adjustment, and signifies the advent of mature postural control.

The child who cannot stay still, instinctively knows that her balance still needs practice. The child who cannot stay on the sidewalk if there is a low wall running alongside it, but who must climb from one level to another and back again, is still teaching herself muscle control, depth perception and visualmotor integration skills. Somersaults and cartwheels further facilitate the separation of motion from other sensations, for it is only when a child has control of movement that she can pay attention to other experiences.

Hyperactivity and Attention Deficit may be two signs of immaturity in vestibular functioning. As parents, teachers and caretakers, we tend to implore our hyperactive children to "sit still" and to "be quiet". It has been shown that hyperactive children who are allowed to spin for 30 seconds in either direction, show increased attention span for up to 30 minutes afterwards, suggesting that they need vestibular stimulation to "get their brain into gear".

Our eyes operate from the vestibular circuit in the brain. Our ears share the same cranial nerve and the sense of touch is integrally linked to the vestibular through the movement across hair cells whose receptors are located in the dermis of the skin. If motion is a child's first language, then sensation is his second. Only when both motion and sensation are integrated can the higher language skills of speech, reading and writing develop fluently. Our children who roll and tumble are engaged in their first lesson toward becoming the Einsteins of the future.

Other Papers and Articles by Sally Goddard Blythe:

1. *The role of primitive survival reflexes in the visual system.* Journal of Behavioral Optometry 6/2 1995 31-35

2. *Baby's first playground.* You and Your Baby Magazine 3/3 1998 113-1

3. *In praise of song and dance.* Times Education Supplement 23.1.98

4. *Music Matters* Music Teacher 9/98

5. *Screening for neurological dysfunction in the specific learning difficulty child* The British Journal of Occupational Therapy 61/10 1998

6. *Why movement matters to your child* Natural Parent Jan/Feb 1999

Appendix 4

Glossary

Accommodation: ability to focus quickly from near to far distance and vice versa.

Afferent: information leading to the brain.

Babkin response: The stimulus for this reflex consists of deep pressure, applied simultaneously to the palms of both hands while the infant is an appropriate position, ideally supine. The stimulus is followed by flexion or forward bowing of the head, opening of the mouth and closing of the eyes. The reflex can be demonstrated in the newborn, but should be inhibited after four months of age. It shows a neurological link between the mouth and the hands, which also becomes obvious in the palming movements of the hands a child makes while nursing. (Kittens do this when being fed.) Like many reflexes, it can be elicited in either direction.

Balance system: monitors all sensation in both directions.

Basal Ganglia: Three small masses of nerve tissue —the caudate nucleus, the putamen and the globus pallidus. Located at the base of the brain, they are involved in the subconscious regulation of movements.

Bradycardia: slow heartbeat rate,

Cephalo-caudal law: from head downward sequel of development in the infant.

Crawling: moving forward using arms and legs with belly and chest on the ground. (Crawling on tummy)

Creeping: crawling on hands and knees.

dB (decibels): measure of volume of sound.

Dermis: Top layer of the skin.

Dominance: Supremacy of one side over another within the brain. This refers to the two cerebral hemispheres, but it can be applied to other parts of the body, where there are two of each. E.g. the hands, ears, eyes, feet. etc.

Dyslexia: Inability to read. Generally used only in cases where there is normal intelligence, but where the usual methods of teaching have failed.

Extension: Movement away from the body.

Efferent: information or commands from the central nervous system to the body.

Figure ground effect: inability to separate and categorize conflicting visual information, e.g. walking up an open staircase or crossing a slatted bridge, where the water can be seen through the boards.

Flexion: bending toward the front center of the body.

Fixation: focusing of eyes on a stationary point and holding that focus.

Hyper: oversensitive, inadequate filtering of extraneous sensations.

Hypertonus: extensor muscles exert greater influence than the flexor muscles.

Hypo: undersensitive -inadequate sensations received.

Hypotonus: weak muscle tone.

Hz: Hertz vibrations per second, determine the pitch of the sound heard. E.g. 125 Hz is low sound, 8000 Hz is perceived as high sound.

In utero: in the mother's womb.

Kinesthesis: see proprioception.

Limbic system: Part of the old cortex and its primary related nuclei. It is shared by all mammals and is associated with smell, autonomic functions and certain aspects of emotion and behavior.

Midbrain: the uppermost part of the brain stem. The term midbrain is sometimes used to include all the structures just below the cortex, sometimes even including the cerebellum.

Muscle tone: balance between flexion and extension muscles.

Myelin: a soft fatty substance surrounding a nerve fiber.

Neuro-developmental delay: The presence of primitive reflexes beyond their normal age of inhibition and/or the absence of postural reflexes.

Opisthotonus: A form of spasm in which the head and heels are bent backward and the body bowed forward.

Parasympathetic nervous system: increases salivary gland secretions, decreases the heart rate, promotes digestion and dilates the blood vessels. It is the opposite partner of the sympathetic nervous system.

Proprioception: ability to know where different parts of the body are and to carry out complex maneuvers without conscious awareness. Though often used interchangeably with kinesthesis, the term proprioception encompasses all sensations involving body position, either at rest or in motion, the term kinesthesia refers only to sensations arising when active muscle contraction becomes involved.

Reflex: involuntary movement in response to a stimulus and the entire physiological process activitating it.

Reflex Inhibition Program: A series of exercises based upon fetal and infant movement patterns. Its purpose is to inhibit aberrant primitive reflexes and is tailored specifically to the needs of each individual.

Reticular Activating System: A complex network of nerve fibers, occupying the central core of the brain stem, that function in wakefullness and alertness.

Simian: ape-like.

Saccades: rapid eye movements which accuratedly take the eye from fixation point to fixation point when a person reads a line of text. Saccadic eye movement also serves the function of erasing the prior visual image.

Scoliosis: abnormal curvature of the spine.

Sympathetic nervous system: network of nerve fibers which, especially under stress, ready the body for either flight or standing to fight. It does so by increasing the heartbeat, quickening the breath and enhancing the supply of oxygen to the muscles by syphoning the blood supply from the skin to deep muscle. It works in a balancing act with the parasympathetic nervous system to keep the body in a state of metabolic equilibrium.

Tactile defensive: touch receptors respond to stimulation as if it were a threat.

Threshold: the point at which a stimulus is strong enough to cross over a synapse.

Ventral: lying or supported on tummy, head and hips not supported.

White noise: continuous background sensation, which is always present andintrudes upon other sensations. Can be an auditory, a visual or a tactile sensation.

INDEX

— NOTES —

For test demonstrations and interview with Peter Blythe and Sally Goddard, the following VHS video is available . . .

LEARNING PROBLEMS AND NEURO-DEVELOPMENTAL DELAY

PETER BLYTHE, Ph.D.
SALLY GODDARD, N.D.T.

"Learning disabled","hyperactive","Attention Deficit Syndrome child" are the lables carelessly attached to any child who does not function well in the classroom. To give these children simply more of the same methods which have failed before, is a waste of time. We must look to see what skills —in hearing, vision and hand-eye coordination— the children lack and then find ways to improve these functions.

Using the recent research which attests to the plasticity of the brain and know-how based on decades of research on the impact of the reflexes on the development of children, the Institute of Neuro-Physiological Psychology has developed a standardized method of evaluating the reflex structure of a child. With the insight gained, they designed a program of intervention that is both easily and inexpensively implemented and individual to the particular needs of the child.

These methods permit not only a precise measurement of what keeps the child from learning or paying attention but allows a clear evaluation of any progress made after the child has completed a home-based program of reflex inhibition, which may take no more than four to twenty minutes a day.

PART I:	Background and Rationale	(35 min.)
PART II:	Reflex Evaluation Techniques and the Impact of the Reflex Structure on Behavior	(30 min.)
PART III:	Case Histories & Controlled Studies	(24 min.)

Produced for Literacy Education and Referral Network
Eugene Public Library, 100 West 13th Ave., Eugene, OR 97401

Send $29.95 U.S. funds for 89 min.VHS copy to:
Fern Ridge Press
1927 McLean Blvd., Eugene, OR 97405 • 541-485-8243 / Fax 541-687-7701

*For video in the **PAL** format contact:*
The Institute for Neuro-Physiological Psychology,
Warwick House, 4 Stanley Place, Chester CH1 2LU, UK
Tel & Fax: 01244311414